LIVING
ON THE
PROPHETIC
EDGE

I0167907

Russ Moyer

WITH A FOREWORD BY
JOSHUA MILLS

Cover design by Miguel Simon

Published by:

McDougal & Associates
18896 Greenwell Springs RD
Greenwell Springs, LA 70739
www.thepublishedword.com

McDougal & Associates is dedicated to spreading the
Gospel of the Lord Jesus Christ to as many people as
possible in the shortest time possible.

ISBN: 978-1-940461-65-6

Printed on demand in the U.S., the U.K., and Australia
For Worldwide Distribution

Presented To:

_____

By:

_____

On:

_____

Message:

_____

_____

_____

_____

FOREWORD
BY JOSHUA MILLS

It is my privilege to recommend to you the ministry of Dr. Russ Moyer and this tremendous book, *Living on the Prophetic Edge*. As I have come to know Brother Russ since we met in 2003, he has become a personal mentor in my life and ministry. It would be absolutely impossible to describe in detail the impact and anointing that has been released into my life, my family and my ministry through the timely prophetic word and powerful realm of revelation that Brother Russ lives and ministers in. Time after time he has spoken the precise word of the Lord, and we have stood in awe to witness it come to pass days, weeks, months or even years later.

Many times I have heard Brother Russ say that his life and ministry is led by the revelation of God through visions, dreams and prophetic understanding. In this book, he begins to outline the supernatural and practical keys the Lord has given him for operating in this unique and unusual gifting.

The Word of God boldly declares *"You may all prophesy ..."* (1 Corinthians 14:31), and I believe this is the heart and spirit behind this book. It is a how-to manual for any believer who desires to operate in greater prophetic ability. Throughout each chapter, you will gain greater insight and grow in the knowledge of Heaven, in order to become a mouthpiece for God in the earth. As you read this book, I believe you will truly experience yourself going from glory to glory!

As I have traveled around the world, ministering in churches, conferences and large events now for more than twenty years, something I have discovered is that the voice of prophecy is one of the most misunderstood, and yet most powerful, tools that God has given to us today. The Scriptures declare that God will do nothing unless He first reveals it through a prophetic utterance in the earth (see Amos 3:7). God is looking for willing vessels who will yield their spirits to the Spirit of Revelation and begin to operate with keen insight, accurate solutions and the remarkable wisdom that is available within the atmosphere of prophetic outpouring.

In your hands, you are holding a life-changing book, filled with personal testimonies, scriptural understanding and divine revelation that will guide you into this arena of hearing the voice of God and participating with that realm. In my personal opinion, Brother Russ Moyer has written one of the greatest prophetic resources I have ever had the ability to obtain.

As you read through the pages of this book, I would encourage you to highlight, underline and make notes throughout, as I believe the Lord will begin speaking to you in great and mighty ways. Expect to hear His voice, anticipate His glory and get ready to begin *Living on the Prophetic Edge!* This is one book you will not want to put down until you have read it from cover to cover!

In His Great Love,
Joshua Mills
International Glory Ministries
Palm Springs, California/London, ON, Canada
www.joshuamills.com

DEDICATION

I want to dedicate this book to the many spiritual sons and daughters God has sent my way. By divine appointment, He establishes golden connections and covenant relationships. My prayer for you is that you would take your gift to the fullest place of fruitfulness.

You are the generation, the prophetic generation, that I believe is called to usher in the Second Coming of the Lord. You're the generation that is called to blow the trumpet in Zion, to sound the alarm. May God rightly connect you together in relationship as end-time warriors and end-time handmaidens in faith transformation.

God bless you!

ACKNOWLEDGMENTS

There are many people who have played a part in this book, not just those who worked so diligently to pull it together, but also those who, for more than thirty-five years, have been there for me as I have tried to live life on the prophetic edge:

- The **former employees** of my businesses who were all birthed in the power and spirit of revelation
- The **members of the Eagle Worldwide Network**
- The **families, ministers, churches and leadership at Eagle Worldwide Ministries**
- The **mentors** and **spiritual prophetic fathers** God has sent my way (such as the late **Ruth Heflin, Paul Wetzel** from Pensacola, Florida and **Jane Lowder** from Calvary Pentecostal Tabernacle and Campgrounds in Ashland, Virginia). They recognized and believed in the gift that God put in my heart and life.

There were many others. Some, in particular, I would like to recognize for their contribution:

- **Pastor Patty Thorpe**, my administrator, who helped me put out the message of this book

- **Miguel Simon,** Vice President of Eagle Worldwide Ministries, who helped with the original cover design and layout and originally formatted *Living on the Prophetic Edge* to send to the printer
- **Nellie Balandowich,** who helped me take it from a teaching format to a book format
- **Victoria Grassick,** who has faithfully helped to proofread this and many other projects
- **My wife, Mave,** who has walked this unusual walk right along with me. I appreciate her so much. She has the tremendous degree of tolerance that's required when you're called to walk with someone who is trying to be led by the Spirit.

ENDORSEMENTS FOR
LIVING ON THE PROPHETIC EDGE

"Dr. Russ Moyer is a modern-day prophet. I have personally traveled with him to many places and experienced how the messages contained in this book have impacted churches, businesses, families and individuals, bearing the fruit of radical transformation.

At our church, we are grateful to Dr. Russ for coming and sharing this message. The Lord has set our church on fire, and signs, wonders and miracles have followed the preaching of this message. Our church has more than doubled since we have fully embraced these teachings. This book was birthed in the heart of God.

ARE YOU HUNGRY? Then read this book and discover keys to unlocking prophetic insights for your life. Learn to hear the voice of God for yourself. Receive a fresh impartation of the gifts of the Spirit. I highly recommend the book to anyone seeking revival and a real move of God."

John Irving
Pastor, The Gathering Place
Aurora, Ontario

"Dr. Russ Moyer's new book, *Living on the Prophetic Edge,* will take you into a greater understanding of the prophetic. It is a realm that is not fully understood in the church world today. However, Dr. Moyer does an excellent job of expounding on this realm and bringing the reader into a greater revelation on the power of the prophetic. After reading this book, you will find yourself *Living on the Prophetic Edge.* May you be blessed as you read it."

Dr. Jane Lowder
Director of Calvary Campground
Ashland, VA

"Russ Moyer is one of the most prophetic men I know! He truly lives what he preaches and writes about. For Russ, the prophetic edge is not just declaring, but also listening attentively for the voice of God.

If you desire to put a sharper edge on the prophetic in your life, this is the book for you. Sit at the feet of a man who knows the heart of God and is declaring a prophetic word for Canada and the nations."

Fred Bennett
Host of "The Bridge"
The Miracle Channel

"*Living on the Prophetic Edge* is an exciting book by Prophet Russ Moyer, a book that will really take you on a journey through the prophetic. Any person who is called to the prophetic will be greatly blessed and educated by it, as it covers the total picture of the prophetic world and the prophetic life.

Having been Dr. Russ Moyer's pastor, I witnessed him giving his first prophecy and then watched him live and grow into the prophet he is today. I can say that Russ Moyer truly lives on the edge and lives out, in his personal life and ministry, every chapter in his book. I am very happy to endorse the book in its entirety. I know you will benefit greatly as you read and digest *Living on the Prophetic Edge*."

Pastor Paul Wetzel
Former Pastor, Courts of Praise Fellowship
Pensacola, FL

"Good stuff! *Living on the Prophetic Edge* is a great read for those wishing to understand the reality and function of true prophetic ministry in the Church, the marketplace and in the world around us. Russ Moyer breaks down the elements of what it takes to truly live on the cutting edge of what God is doing and saying today.

I highly recommend the book to those who want to increase their understanding of spiritual truths and walk in the reality of the Word of God."

Charlie Robinson
President, Revival Canada Christian Ministries

CONTENTS

Foreword by Joshua Mills...5

Introduction...17

1. Living on the Edge 21

2. Prophetic Protocol 28

3. The How, When, Where, Why and Why Not
   of the Prophetic 37

4. Hearing the Voice of the Lord 45

5. Eleven Channels of Prophecy...................................60

6. The Many Gifts of the Spirit and Their Use 70

7. Prophetic Streams 88

8. A New Dimension of Kingdom Revelation 93

9. The Song of the Lord.. 101

10. Poetic Prophecy.. 109

11. Prophetic Proclamation and Declaration.............. 118

12. Relationships: the Prophet, the People and the Lord....... 124

13. The Role of the Prophetic Voice in the Marketplace 132

14. Prophetic Intercession 139

15. Learning to Operate in the Visionary Realm 146

16. Understanding End-Time Prophecy 1154

17. Practicing and Teaching Prophetic Worship 160

18. Your Prophetic Journey to Destiny 167

19. My Own Burden for Discipleship and Mentoring.... 182

20. Catching a Fresh Revelation of the Lord 189

21. This Time and Season 196

22. The Importance of Spiritual Gates and Gatekeepers 202

23. Where Are My Elijahs? 209

Bibliography 215

Author Contact Page 216

INTRODUCTION

Living on the Prophetic Edge was first birthed in my spirit while I was doing a monthly series of online prophetic teachings. The title is a description of the life I have lived since 1977, when the Lord touched my heart and changed my life with a powerful personal encounter. My wife, Mave, says that if you're not living on the edge, then you're taking up too much space in the Kingdom.

I have found that this prophetic life and prophetic call continually challenge me to the very edge of myself. God is ever calling us into deeper water. He is, as we know, *"the same yesterday, today and forever,"* but His mercies are *"new every morning."* Living a life in the prophetic is exciting beyond description, a life of faith, being led by the Spirit.

The Spirit is even now calling us to deeper and deeper places. To every one of His children, but particularly to this prophetic generation, it is deep crying out unto deep.

I was ordained, trained and mentored in my prophetic gift by a fabulous apostolic prophet of God, Ruth Heflin. She was a prophetess to the nations, and she prophesied and ministered in virtually every nation of the world before her glorious homecoming in September of 2000. I had the opportunity to spend much of that last year with her,

Jane Lowder and so many other strong prophetic leaders at Calvary Pentecostal Tabernacle and Campground in Ashland, Virginia.

It was a time of a powerful move of the Spirit of God, and people visited the camp both during the winter and summer campmeetings, from many other nations of the world. To see the gifts of the Spirit, and particularly the power of prophecy, in action was like a breath of fresh air for me. I had just finished nearly three years in Pensacola, Florida at the Brownsville Revival School of Ministry and was able to participate in the great Pensacola Outpouring. Still, the Lord had spoken to me audibly and through dreams and visions, with prophetic confirmations, that Ashland was the place I was to go for prophetic mentoring.

When I first stepped onto the Ashland campground, the Lord said to me, "This is holy ground." He told me that I had just stepped into deeper waters, and WOW, had I ever. In the days to come, I learned much about myself and about my gift and calling.

Through more than twenty years in business and ministry, I had walked through an educational process of learning to hear God's voice and to yield and submit to His will. But that year at Ashland gave me an opportunity to see the power of God in action in a practical way and to interact and fellowship with other prophetic people.

Until then, I had often wondered if I might not be a little strange. I seemed to find it hard, at times, to fit into the typical Christian and church setting. In Ashland, I felt right at home. Just seeing, hearing and experiencing the power, the presence and the glory of God in such a dramatic way changed my Christian perspective. I learned so much.

Two things in particular that Sister Ruth said to me in those days have stayed with me to this very moment:

1.   The first one was: "Brother, if you don't know what to say, just prophesy. God always knows what to say."

In her books, *River Glory* and *Revelation Glory*, she spoke of the River of God. She knew about the river, she knew about the glory, and she knew about hearing the voice of the Lord. She had a walking, talking, living relationship with Him, and, therefore, when you heard her prophesy, it seemed like all of Heaven had suddenly come down to Earth.

2.   The second unforgettable thing she said to me was: "Every time you step into the River of God, you step into a new place in the river."

My purpose for writing *Living on the Prophetic Edge* is so that this prophetic generation might find a place to connect and feel accepted. I believe there is a call on my life is to raise up and empower this prophetic generation. Before Ashland, I found that, in my own life, there was a huge void of instruction and teaching in this regard that was practical, that could show me how to apply my gift to every area of my life and ministry.

Part of my call, therefore, is to restore the gift of prophecy and the office of the prophet back to the Body of Christ. If that is to happen, it must be done with integrity, proper protocol and understanding of spiritual authority. The fathers and mothers in the Spirit must rise up and take their rightful place, to mentor this emerging prophetic community.

I believe that, in addition to the teaching of this book there will be a strong impartation taking place as I pray at the end of each chapter and believe God to empower you, imparting to you and activating you, not just in your gift and calling, but in a prophetic life and lifestyle, so that you, too, may experience *Living on the Prophetic Edge.*

Russ Moyer
Canada and the U.S.

Chapter 1

LIVING ON THE EDGE

Jeremiah 29:11, NIV

"For I know the plans I have for you," declares the LORD, "Plans to prosper you and not to harm you, plans to give you a hope and a future."

God wants to take each of us to a place of *Living on the Prophetic Edge*, but we must be willing to go there. When the Lord saved you and called you, it was not so that you could live a mediocre life, just warm a pew, or live the *status quo*. His love for us and His plans for us are much greater than that. Jeremiah declared it.

That is not to say it will be easy. It requires a lifetime of learning to hear God's voice and obey Him, as His ways are not our ways. His ways are much higher than ours. Therefore, He calls us up, to go beyond the veil, to enter into a life of faith. In this chapter, I want to talk to you about what it means to live on the edge in our faith in every way.

What is God looking for in us? There is a uniqueness that God has given you. His DNA is imprinted upon you, and He knows how to speak to you in ways you will understand. He would not speak to someone else the same way as to you. Still, in everything that He does, He never contradicts His character nor His Word.

Today the walls of denominationalism are coming down, and God is raising up a people who are bold, who are equipped, who hear His voice and who do not fear man. He is raising up people who will advance His Kingdom and bring that Kingdom to Earth, and this requires taking our faith to the limit and beyond. There are no limits in God. May the Lord open the eyes of our understanding as we go about doing the Father's business.

Living on the Prophetic Edge ... that is really what it is all about. This means living in the Spirit, being led by the Spirit of God. Romans 8:14 declares:

For as many are led by the Spirit of God, they are the sons of God.

The Bible also tells us to live by the Spirit and when we do, we will not fulfill the lusts of the flesh (see Galatians 5:16).

Living on the Prophetic Edge ... I'm talking about the apostolic edge, under the breaker anointing, taking it to the limit, living, ruling and reigning in the fullness of the Spirit, knowing the power and authority that has been given to us and taking it to the limit for the Kingdom, with the purpose of extending and advancing that Kingdom.

When we come to the edge of ourselves, we come to the only place where man can meet God, and that is a place called faith. This is living by faith.

Our justification is only through faith. *"The just shall live by faith,"* not leaning on their own understanding, but leaning on the Lord, living according to His Word, living by the Spirit.

This word *kingdom* is a governmental term. You and I need to know that we are not governed by the powers of this world, nor by the natural principles established in the mind of man. Our authority comes from a higher power, a higher authority than anything in this world.

When men asked Jesus about this, He told them that His Kingdom and authority were *"not of this world"* (John 18:36). When His disciples asked Him to teach them to pray, He gave them what we commonly refer to as The Lord's Prayer. In that model prayer, He said we should pray, *"Thy kingdom come, Thy will be done, on earth as it is in heaven"* (Matthew 6:10). God is looking for Heaven to touch Earth, in order to extend the King's dominion. And you and I are called to be ambassadors for Christ.

Myles Munroe said that the Holy Spirit is the Governor of God's Kingdom on Earth. He is extending His Kingdom, and we are His prophetic agents, His voice and His hands on Earth. Jesus' heart was to do only what He saw the Father do and only say what He heard the Father saying. He didn't just hear in the natural, and He didn't just speak in the natural. He could hear the Father by the power of the Spirit.

We need to stop bowing our knee to man and start bowing to the King of Kings and the Lord of Lords. To be led by the Spirit and live by the Spirit ... that is the purpose of the Church. When I say that I am talking about The Church, not a local fellowship or a denomination. We are much bigger than that. We are the Church of the Lord Jesus Christ.

In the New Testament, the book of Acts speaks of three primary church centers, fellowships or churches. There was the Church at Jerusalem, the Church at Ephesus and the Church at Antioch. Because of persecution, the Church at Jerusalem was scattered. Only the apostles remained in Jerusalem. It is my belief that this had a godly purpose. God sent these believers out to do His work in other places. If that is true, why would He leave the apostles in Jerusalem? I believe it was to sit in counsel.

This worked out for the best. If He had sent these leaders out, they might have wanted to circumcise every new male believer and turn them all into Jews, with the same religious and legalistic attitudes. This could have hindered the development of the Church. We need to make sure that we are not doing the same thing today, for we are neither Jew nor Greek, neither bond nor free (see Galatians 3:28). It's all about being one new man in Christ, letting go of the things that are behind and reaching toward the goal, the high call in Christ Jesus.

Our God is a God of individuality, not a cookie-cutter

God. He does not want all of us to look alike, dress alike and talk alike. He anoints people like you and me, those with no recognizable name, no recognizable face and no preconceived agenda. Our agenda must be His agenda.

Think about Elijah:

James 5:17-18

Elias was a man subject to like passions as we are, and he prayed earnestly that it might not rain, and it rained not on the earth by the space of three years and six months. And he prayed again and the heaven gave rain, and the earth brought forth her fruit.

If you are a Catholic minister today, you have to wear a collar or a robe, and if you are a Baptist, Pentecostal or Protestant, you can't do that. Personally, I don't care if you're doing laps around the building or sitting solemnly in your pew. God looks at the heart. It seems that we have a constant urge for conformity. If you go to a casual church today, everyone has to wear jeans or shorts, or you're not free. How can that be? What happened to freedom of expression? I am what I am. Do I have to worship just like you or work just like you? Or am I legitimately free to be me?

Worship is a posture of the heart, and freedom has nothing to do with prison walls. We erect too many walls through conformity, religion and legalism. If you have been set free by the Son, then you are free indeed. Period!

Sometimes, when we go to a church where people dress casual and everyone else is in jeans, we feel condemned, as if everyone considers us to be religious for dressing another way. The one who is religious is the one who conforms for the sake of conformity, rather than being led by the Spirit and the joy in their heart.

What does the Church at Ephesus represent? I believe that it is the emerging church. The book of Ephesians describes a church coming out of spiritual warfare, a five-fold ministry church, a place of intimacy, revelation, wisdom and understanding. Revelation chapters 2 through 4 are about spiritual authority and about church government and the proper leadership structure.

The Church at Antioch was the first place where believers were called Christians, meaning "little Christs." The entire work of the Holy Spirit is to make us more like Jesus. This was His heart for us as well. In His prophetic word given in John 14:12, He said that we would do greater works than He had done:

Verily, verily, I say unto you, he that believeth on me, the works that I do shall he do also; and greater works than these shall he do; because I go to my Father.

The church at Antioch was a multi-ethnic, multi-cultural, multi-gifted gathering made up of prophets and teachers, like Lucius and Niger. Then there was Saul, later Paul, the Jew, the Pharisees of Pharisees, and Barnabas, the businessman and great encourager. It was this church that sent these two men out to fulfill their apostolic missionary calling.

If we are going to be an apostolic church, we have to be a sending church. Today, my prayer for you is that you would begin *Living on the Prophetic Edge*, that you will allow the Lord to launch you fully and wholly into the harvest. I send you as He sent me, and as the Father sent Christ. Let us be about the Father's business.

Father, thank You for saving us and calling us. Thank You for the destiny You have given each one of us. Father, I pray that the eyes of our understanding would be opened to all that You have for us and that we would comprehend true freedom in You. Father, that we would see with Your eyes and be Your voice in the earth, that we would not fear man, but be led by Your Spirit, that we would know the freedom and fulfillment of living on the prophetic edge in our faith.

In Jesus' name,
Amen!

Chapter 2

PROPHETIC PROTOCOL

1 Corinthians 12:1

Now concerning spiritual gifts, brethren, I would not have you to be ignorant.

1 Corinthians 14:40

Let all things be done decently and in order.

Everywhere I go, I share the message of prophetic protocol because of the mandate God has given me in restoring the prophetic to its proper function within the corporate Body. In my travels, and in having planted ten churches under Eagle Worldwide Ministries, I have found that knowing when, where, who and how is key to proper procedure, to be able to minister prophetically in a way that honors the Lord and His people.

There is much misunderstanding when it comes to the prophetic. The Bible reveals that every Christian can hear from God, and that you *"may all prophesy"* (1 Corinthians 14:31). However, we must learn the different functions of prophecy and how this gift works in the local church and among the corporate Body.

In this chapter, I will explain the difference between the prophetic gifting and the office of the prophet and the realm of responsibility that office carries. If you receive a prophetic word from the Lord, and you are not in your local church, how should you bring that word forth? How would you react if you were told you could not bring it forth? The following is a guideline for the operation of the prophetic, so that everything is done "*decently and in order.*"

We can point the finger to a number of areas to identify why it has not yet happened. For instance, we could point to pastors, to decisions made by denominations and to the work of religious spirits. But, even though I am myself a prophetic voice, I have to admit that the blame lies, first and foremost, with a lack of integrity and an unwillingness to submit to spiritual authority on the part of many prophetic people of today and in former times as well. Many in our churches have been hurt by what we call the "Parking Lot Prophet," and so has the prophetic ministry in general.

In addition to walking in the office of a prophet, I have, in some seasons of ministry, pastored a church and I believe that every prophetic person should serve, at some point, in leadership and pastoral care, so that they can gain an understanding of the awesome responsibility a pastor faces when trying to protect the men and women the Lord has put in their charge.

When Paul began his teaching concerning spiritual gifts in 1 Corinthians 12-14, he stated in 12:1:

Now concerning spiritual gifts, brethren, I would not have you to be ignorant

Paul ended that particular teaching in 14:40 with this admonition:

Let all things be done decently and in order.

These are both key verses to the operation of the prophetic in the Church, which was the heart of Paul's teaching. In order for us to truly operate effectively in the gift of prophecy, we need some good solid teaching that brings true understanding to the use and function of the prophetic gift in the Church, and we must emphasize again and again that, in the use and operation of the prophetic gift, everything must be done decently and in order.

There is a difference between the gift of prophecy and the office of a prophet, and there is also a different realm of responsibility and authority between the two. Not everyone who prophesies is a prophet, but every prophet prophesies. The office of the prophet carries much more power and authority, but also, someone who is in the office of a prophet is more recognized and holds some form of leadership role.

In addition to prophesying, prophets raise up other people in their gifting, through both training and impartation. Many times prophets lead or are part of a prophetic company and are recognized as such. A prophet can lay hands on another prophet, imparting into them and mentoring them, just as Elijah did with Elisha. A prophet can also lay hands on and anoint a king or other government leader, as Samuel did with King David.

A prophet may prophesy direction, both to individuals and to the whole Church body, and, occasionally, can bring correction in love. In both Old and New Testament times, prophets declared judgment. Also, as noted in Acts 13, prophets can, at the prompting of the Holy Spirit, lay hands on, anoint and launch ministers into their assignments and calling, as was done with Barnabas and Saul.

An individual who moves in the gift of prophecy and not the office gift of the prophet must adhere to the New Testament model for the prophetic:

1 Corinthians 14:3

But he that prophesieth speaketh unto men to edification, and exhortation, and comfort.

All individuals who operate in the gift of prophecy or in the office of a prophet must come to understand that when they come into a church, a fellowship or any meeting of believers, there is a God-ordained leader for that house, most often called the pastor. If we intend to operate in our gifting, we must operate under the proper spiritual authority God has ordained for that house.

Personally, if I feel that I will be operating in my gift, I must make myself known to that pastor and see if that particular congregation is open to having someone bring a prophetic utterance. If so, what do they consider the proper timing for the use of that gift? You can only imagine how a pastor might feel if someone comes to his meeting that he doesn't know, and they stand up in the middle of the service and begin to belt out a word, possibly even of gloom and doom, over the Lord's people whom he is responsible for protecting. How would you feel? I know how I would feel, and my next move would be to call on the ushers to remove the individual who didn't have enough spiritual understanding or maturity to utilize his gift decently and in order.

If we are to be recognized and effective at bringing the gift back into the Body, we will have to work together closely—the pastor and the prophet—respecting one another and our giftings, callings and responsibilities. There is a commanded blessing in unity, and many times people utilizing their gift in a disorderly manner (with the wrong timing or in the wrong way) bring confusion. And we know that the Holy Spirit is not the author of confusion (see 1 Corinthians 14:3).

Over the last ten years, I have raised up more than a hundred prophetic voices and launched them into their gifting and calling, and the churches that I am involved with have developed some simple, but precise guidelines for the use and operation of the gift of prophecy.

First, whenever possible, we have a microphone which faces the people. That is a good indication to a prophetic person that would come to our fellowship that we *want* to hear the word of the Lord spoken through God's people.

Second, when an individual receives a word, if they are known and released to bring a prophetic word in our church, they come to the front and ask permission from the leader in authority, normally having written out the word they wish to share. That leader, in turn, will release them by giving them a microphone, but still they must wait for the right timing.

If this occurs during worship, the person wishing to share a word with the congregation will wait for the worship leader to break and acknowledge them before they deliver their word. If this word, in the opinion of the leader, would fit better in a different part of the service, they will indicate that and then call the individual up at a later time. Perhaps the word this person has received has to do with the offering, or perhaps it would confirm the preaching of the Word or would fit more appropriately during ministry time. This would be true if it is, for instance, a word of knowledge about an illness or disease that the Lord wants to heal.

During our services, for the most part, we only entertain corporate words and not individual words, other than by the designated speaker for that service or the person who is in authority over the service.

When delivering a word, we must all, as the Bible tells us concerning sounding a trumpet, make sure that it is not *"an uncertain sound* [an unclear signal]"(1 Corinthians 14:8). What does this mean? It means the following:

Speak as clearly as you can, trying not to speak too fast, because the Lord wants everyone in attendance to clearly hear and understand what He is saying.

Start when the Spirit starts, stop when the Spirit stops, and don't take away or add to the word the Lord has given you.

Try to catch the tempo of the Spirit and the timing of the service. If I have an upbeat word of encouragement or exhortation, I will probably want to bring it during the praise portion of the service. If it is a consoling word or a word that is emotionally deep, having to do with the heart and the love of the Lord, I will probably want to bring it during the worship part of the service, when the hearts of the Lord's people are open to hearing it better.

It is God's desire that, from the first sound (the opening moment of a service), everything continues to build, so that when I bring a word, that word must always take the service higher, never lower. We have all been in services when the anointing on the service had built to a certain point, and then someone came out with a deadpan delivery or a word that had heaviness all over it, and it brought the entire congregation to a lower spiritual place, rather than to a higher place.

God's will is for us to continually go higher. Therefore, do your best to sense the tempo of the Spirit and the timing of God. The anointing, at times, is like a wave, and when I'm delivering a word, I want to catch the wave and allow the anointing to bring the service to a higher level.

And, finally, concerning delivery: I want to try my very best not to bring attention to myself, but rather to draw attention to the word of the Lord. At times, there may be a strong internal anointing that makes me want to manifest, but *"the spirits of the prophets are subject to the prophets"* (1 Corinthians 14:32), and I want to do my very best to deliver that word clearly, precisely, and with as much attention to the word itself as possible.

As soon as I am finished, I want to hand the microphone back to the person in authority, go to my seat and thank God in my heart that He chose to share His heart with me and through me in this way.

Let me close this chapter with this thought: I have had many personal experiences in which the Lord gave me a word and I brought it to those in authority, but, for one reason or another, they decided they didn't want me to deliver it or deliver it right then. This is when you discover the depth of maturity and character of an individual. Being a prophetic voice, being a prophetic person is all about how you act and how you react. Do you stomp off, go back to your seat, pout, criticize or complain to someone else? Are you mature enough to realize that when you go forward and share what the Lord has spoken to you, you have done your job? This is a test. It is a test for the leader, and it is a test for you and me too.

Pass the test, knowing that every test is a wonderful opportunity for promotion. God is much more interested in our character, in how much of the fruit of the Spirit is in our lives than He is in the gifts we might possess.

I hope that these few points will help you as you seek the Lord in pursuing your gifting and calling. You and I are responsible to be the generation that brings the prophetic voice back into the Church. If it is to happen, it will require integrity, character and submission to authority, so that all things can be done *"decently and in order."*

Father, I pray an impartation of the prophetic gifting upon all my readers. I pray also, Lord, for the gift of wisdom and revelation to be imparted to them. I pray for discernment to rest upon them. Lord, I pray that they would be sensitive to Your Holy Spirit, as they are equipped and prepared to move prophetically, as they devote themselves to You and mature, and as the prophetic is being restored to Your Church.

In Jesus name,
Amen!

Chapter 3

THE HOW, WHEN, WHERE, WHY AND WHY NOT OF THE PROPHETIC

1 Corinthians 12:1

Now concerning spiritual gifts, brethren, I would not have you to be ignorant.

1 Corinthians 14:40

Let all things be done decently and in order.

The following is a blueprint of the how, when, where, why and why not of the prophetic. As we have seen, it is important for us to understand what was written by Paul and inspired by the Holy Spirit about the proper protocol of the prophetic. It is also important for us to understand that, within the local church, we must submit our gift to the established leadership. In Chapter 2, Prophetic Protocol, we established the basic protocol. Now let's build on that.

Our heavenly Father is a God of perfect timing. He is never early, and neither is He ever late. He is not the

Author of confusion, but, rather, of order. We are to be led by the Spirit and to learn to walk within the parameters He has given us. And we must always remember that the focus is not to be on us, but on the Lord.

Again, the apostle Paul gave us one of the most condensed and yet thorough teachings on the gifts of the Spirit in 1 Corinthians 12. He began by saying that we should not be *"ignorant"* concerning these matters and ended with the all-important admonition: *"Let all things be done decently and in order."*

The chapter numbers and verses in the Bible, as we all know, were not in the original teaching and were only put there later by men as a point of reference. It was basically all one teaching. What can we conclude from this? First, that God wants us to be knowledgeable concerning the spiritual gifts.

In chapter 12, Paul discussed the nine signature gifts of the Spirit, as well as the diversity of operations and administrations of those gifts. He gave us a wonderful analogy concerning the gifts, the human body and the Body of Christ. He also spoke of the five-fold ministry gifts. He ended that part in verse 31, telling us, *"Covet earnestly the best gifts."*

This word *covet* is a very strong word. *The World Book Dictionary* [5] defines it in this way: "To desire earnestly, to wish for especially, or to eagerly long for." Then Paul spent the entirety of chapter 13 speaking of the value and

5. World Book, Inc.: 2015

need for God's kind of love to be used or applied to the use of your gift, and he referred to that in 12:31 as *"a more excellent way."*

Of all of the gifts he had spoken of, Paul then entered into chapter 14 and spent the entirety of that chapter talking to us about one gift, the gift of prophecy. In verse 1, he said:

Follow after charity, and desire spiritual gifts, but rather that ye may prophesy.

This was the desire of Paul but also the desire of God—that you and I would prophesy.

In verse 3 of that chapter, Paul gives us a New Testament model for prophecy:

But he that prophesieth speaketh unto men to edification, and exhortation, and comfort.

He then ends the chapter with verse 40:

Let all things be done decently and in order.

Throughout this chapter, Paul touched on many important areas of this subject. We might say that he covered the how, the when, the where, the why and the why not of the prophetic. I want to encourage you to re-read chapter 14 with the understanding of Paul's emphasis on this very important end-time gift. Now, let's talk about the how of the prophetic.

THE HOW OF THE PROPHETIC

In addition to 1 Corinthians 14:40, where Paul emphasizes order and discipline, we are also shown, in 1 and 2 Chronicles, that the House of the Lord must be set in order; in 2 Samuel 17, that our house needs to be in order. Again, in 2 Kings 20:1 and Isaiah 38:1, the Lord exhorts us: "*SET THINE HOUSE IN ORDER.*"

Our God is a God of order and discipline, and everything He establishes is according to divine order in the universe. He is not the author of confusion; the enemy is the author of confusion. Lack of order always brings us to a place of chaos and anarchy, which are the enemies of God. Paul had a thorough understanding of divine authority and divine order.

When we are operating in the gifts of the Spirit, particularly an end-time gift, such as the gift of prophecy, we must do it in proper alignment and proper order. Paul detailed that proper order in these teachings. They can be generally applied to the gift of prophecy, wherever and whenever a member of the Body is operating in their gifting.

Additionally, in every local church, fellowship or body, there is a local headship, a leader who will establish the protocol for any particular gathering. Therefore, when I feel led to operate in my gift, I must always submit that gift to the established leadership of the local body, I must prophesy in the time allotted (or in appropriate placement), and I must do it with the approval of that established leadership.

Whenever possible, I try to have the prophetic words I release recorded, so that they may be judged and tested (see 1 Corinthians 14:29). If I bring a prophetic word to an individual, I like to have it recorded so that he or she may bring it to their pastor or spiritual leader for further discernment and direction. This also enables the individual to be able to sit down and review that word for further understanding and application.

Because of all this, I try my best to adhere to the following eight rules when I deliver a prophetic word:

1. I use a digital recorder.
2. I seek approval or permission from the governing authority.
3. I find the appropriate timing for the most effective delivery.
4. I try to be sure the word brings edification, comfort and/or encouragement.
5. I try not to bring unneeded attention to myself.
6. I never pout if my word is not received.
7. I stand ready for my word to be judged.
8. I start when the Spirit starts, and I stop when the Spirit stops.

THE WHEN OF THE PROPHETIC

I like to deliver a word in the right timing of a given service. A word should be given as we ascend from praise, to worship, to the glory. It should never bring the service down. It should always bring the Body to a higher level of faith and expectancy.

Because the word must fit into the flow of the service and never out of order, I bring a word forth when the Spirit of the Lord says to. That way, I am not moved by my emotions or led by my soul. As the Scriptures so aptly put it:

Zechariah 4:6
Not by might, nor by power, but by my spirit, saith the LORD of hosts.

THE WHERE OF THE PROPHETIC

Where? In the sanctuary, not in the parking lot. Parking-lot prophets have done a great deal of harm to the Body of Christ. I try to deliver my word in the right setting and under the proper authority.

Can it be done in a restaurant or other public place? Yes, I believe that we are to be utilizing our gifts outside the four walls of the building. The church is not a place; it is you and I. Again, it depends on the circumstances.

I will not deliver a word I feel within me to someone who is in the church, if I am not first released to do it in that particular body. Just because I happen to be sitting in a restaurant setting afterward, still doesn't mean that

I am released. Either I *am* released or I *am not* released.

I much prefer to deliver a word in front of the whole church or at the microphone, not from my seat (unless that is the protocol of the house). The reason is that it's important for all to hear and be edified.

THE WHY OF THE PROPHETIC

Why the prophetic? So that we can be effective in our gifting, so that we can bring acceptance to ourselves and to the word we bear and bring glory to God and not shame. Our gift is to glorify the Lord and therefore must be protected by the spiritual covering in the house.

THE WHY NOT OF THE PROPHETIC

I did mention I was going to share with you the "why not." Why not just do it my own way—whenever and wherever I feel like it? Because I believe that our lack of tact and protocol has caused a lot of problems in the Body of Christ. Many churches and denominations that I visit have been so hurt by Lone Rangers and Smoking Guns, Loose Cannons in the prophetic, that the bulk of what I do in the early stages of my visit is to re-establish confidence and integrity.

Since 1948, we have enjoyed a season of restoration in the Church, with the five-fold ministries being restored and the gifts of the Spirit being restored to the Body, particularly the gift of prophecy and the office gift of the prophet. Part of the responsibility of each of us who have been given divine authority in the prophetic is the burden of operating in and restoring this gift in the way that we can be effective. This is so that God's people can be encouraged and edified, that each prophetic word can be fully received, and that God can be glorified in the way we operate in that gift, cooperating and fellowshipping in the Body and with its leaders.

Lord, I pray that we would hear Your voice and Your voice alone. I pray that the Body of Christ will gain an understanding through Your Word of the importance of the restoration of the prophetic voice in Your Church today, and that they will have a thorough understanding of divine authority and divine order. Thank You, Lord, for teaching us to operate in the gifts of the Spirit.

In Jesus' name,
Amen!

Chapter 4

HEARING THE VOICE OF THE LORD

Romans 8:14

For as many as are led by the Spirit of God, they are the sons of God.

There are many voices that are trying to get your attention in this hour. This is a season to have your ear tuned to the heartbeat of God. It is a time, more than ever before in history, to know the diverse and creative ways God speaks to us. We must be able to discern God's voice above the cares of the day, during the perilous times of our lives as well as during the good times. In *every* season of our lives, we need to hear God's voice for ourselves.

We need a balance. So we need to be grounded in what God is saying in His Word and also by His Spirit. We need to know what God has to say about what is going on around us, so that we do not look to what the world is saying, or even what our situations would seem to speak to us. Now, more than ever before, we must call forth those things that are not as though they were.

In this chapter, I want to give you an overview of some of the ways we can hear from God. He is a wonderful God and knows exactly how to speak to us. He knows what it is that will get our attention and He teaches us to nurture that communication He is developing with us. Let us posture ourselves to hear His voice, knowing that He is able to speak to us in many different ways.

One of the most important experiences for every Christian in this hour, and even more so, for every person who understands that they have a call to the prophetic ministry, is to learn to hear the voice of the Lord.

As we have seen, Paul wrote to the Roman believers:

Romans 8:14

For as many as are led by the Spirit of God, they are the sons of God.

Paul also prayed what to me is one of the most important apostolic prayers recorded in the Scriptures:

Ephesians 1:17-18

That the God of our Lord Jesus Christ, the Father of glory, may give unto you the spirit of wisdom and revelation in the knowledge of him: the eyes of your understanding being enlightened; that ye may know what is the hope of his calling, and what the riches of the glory of his inheritance in the saints.

I believe this is exactly what we need in order to appropriately understand how to hear the voice of the Lord. We need revelation, wisdom and understanding. Revelation is the method, or channel, the Lord chooses to use to reveal His purposes to us. The following are a list of ways the Lord has chosen to speak to me.

THROUGH HIS WORD

God speaks through His Word, and when He does, His Word comes alive for us. He also confirms His Word with signs following. No matter how He speaks to me, one of the most important aspects of my hearing the voice of the Lord is that I bring it back to the Word, to confirm the source and know that I have heard from God.

God is the same yesterday, today and forever, but He is doing new things and saying new things all the time. He puts His finger on a revelation and it becomes a *rhema* word. By His Spirit, the Word is illuminated for right now, and that makes the Word come alive for us personally, *"for such a time as this."*

God may be speaking new things to us individually or personally, but He will not contradict His Word, so I test the spirit and I test the word, going back to the *"more sure"* Word of God.

THROUGH DREAMS AND VISIONS

God certainly speaks to us through dreams and visions. He promised that when Peter quoted the prophet Joel:

Acts 2:17-18

And it shall come to pass in the last days, saith God, I will pour out of my Spirit upon all flesh: and your sons and your daughters shall prophesy, and your young men shall see visions, and your old men shall dream dreams: and on my servants and on my handmaidens I will pour out in those days of my Spirit; and they shall prophesy.

It seem that He didn't leave anyone out. It is His will that everyone hear His voice and be able to prophesy. God said through Job:

Job 33:14-16

For God speaketh once, yea twice, yet man perceiveth it not. In a dream, in a vision of the night, when deep sleep falleth upon men, in slumberings upon the bed; then he openeth the ears of men, and sealeth their instruction.

Throughout the Word, from the beginning right to the end, God used dreams and visions and the revelatory realm to communicate with His people for personal direction and personal guidance. He did it with Paul in Acts16, when He gave him the Macedonia vision. He also guides nations in this way, just as He spoke to Moses and through Moses to the children of Israel, to deliver them from the hand of Pharaoh. The prophetic voice that He wants to use today, to guide the Church and keep us from falling into the pitfalls of this world, are often inspired by dreams and visions.

Numbers 12:6

Hear now my words: If there be a prophet among you,
I the LORD will make myself known to him in a vision,
and will speak unto him in a dream.

God speaks to us in dreams in the deep of the night, but also in the slumberings upon our beds. He knows the right moments, justs before you fall asleep and just after you wake up. Fix your heart on the Lord. Communicate with Him, and then quiet your spirit before Him. Listen to the Lord instead of to self, and Job 33 will come alive for you.

Sometimes God speaks to us in open visions and open revelations. This is when you actually see it or actually hear it in the realm of reality, the natural realm. A closed vision is when you see it or hear it only in the Spirit.

THROUGH AN AUDIBLE VOICE

The audible voice of the Lord is an open revelation, and many people think that is the only way God speaks. From the day I was first baptized in the Spirit in 1976, I have heard the Lord nearly every day and every night when I pray and when I sleep, but I have heard His audible voice only a handful of times. When He uses this method, He does so for serious impact, such as when He declared at the baptism of Jesus, *"This is my beloved Son, in whom I am well pleased"* (Matthew 3:17). Let us open our hearts to every way the Lord can speak to us, for He desires to communicate with us intimately.

I can hear God as clearly during a walk in the park (when all of nature is declaring His glory) as I can on a busy street corner, in the midst of a meeting, or during a trial or tribulation in my life. If I just tune in. I can set my spiritual channel to the channel of the Spirit and plug into His power. In this way, I gain access to a whole revelatory realm. Why should I settle for less, when the whole earth and all the heavens declare His glory?

THROUGH HIS STILL, SMALL VOICE

This is the method the Lord uses most often to speak to us. We get a witness in our Spirit or a check in our Spirit, or we know in our hearts that we have heard from Him directly. However, this is also the area where we are most challenged for discernment. It is fairly easy to tell the voice of the enemy from the voice of God, but it is much more difficult to know whether it is me and my own thoughts or whether these thoughts are actually coming from God.

THROUGH PREACHING AND TEACHING

Jesus was anointed to preach (see Luke 4:18). When someone is anointed to preach, this means that the Holy Spirit takes the Word they preach and amplifies it in the heart of the listener, clarifying it as well. Two people can listen to the same message, and they will come away with very different points. The reason is that the Spirit hones in on the need of the listener and ministers to that need.

THROUGH PROPHETIC VOICES

2 Peter 1:21

For the prophecy came not in old time by the will of man: but holy men of God spake as they were moved by the Holy Ghost.

God speaks through both personal and corporate prophecy, using individuals who operate through the gift of prophecy according to 1 Corinthians 12. This gift is available to all believers. At other times, He moves through men and women who are in a place of leadership in the office gift of the prophet, according to Ephesians 4:11. You can often tell when the office gift is in operation because of its depth, accuracy and authority in sound and decree. Personally, I never move on the word of another man. I want to hear the voice of the Lord for myself and have the prophetic voice and prophetic word only as confirmation.

THROUGH PHYSICAL FEELINGS

Sometimes, when I am preaching or when I am preoccupied mentally or emotionally with a specific task or function, the Lord will speak to me in a physical feeling in my body. Sometimes this is a word of knowledge that God wants to heal someone. *"He sent his word, and healed them"* (Psalm 107:20). I have had times when I felt so out of sorts that I couldn't do something that I actually wanted to do, and I discovered that the Lord was trying to alter my path, my steps and my choices.

For example, I had a friend who had a physical symptom in his body, so significant that he went to the doctor for treatment. The doctor found that the man had something totally unrelated to the original symptoms. The Lord had prompted him with the original symptoms so that he could be treated for a more threatening condition.

THROUGH OUR EMOTIONS

Many times God speaks to me through my emotional feelings, perhaps because I'm not really fully in tune or paying attention. Sometimes I walk into a meeting and feel depressed (and I'm not given to depression, moodiness or anger). When this happens, I am sensing the spirit that is in the house, and God is using my gift of discernment of spirits to do spiritual warfare. This can be during intercession or deliverance, or God will be leading me to prophetically speak, identifying what spirit we need to fight against and how we are to fight it.

Paul prayed that we would have a Spirit of understanding as well. We need to have understanding and knowledge about the way God speaks, but also about how to interpret what He is saying to us. Many times the Lord speaks to us in allegories, symbols, colors and parables. When He speaks in symbols, it goes beyond our natural language.

If you see the symbol on the door to a men's room or ladies' room, you may not understand English, but you recognize the purpose of that symbol. Other examples include the handicap symbol or the universal symbols for traffic signs. Symbolic interpretation, many times, transcends our natural languages, and the Lord speaks to us in those ways.

When I receive any revelation from the Lord, a dream or a vision, for example, I write it down what I saw and the date. Then I bring it back to God, praying it back to Him and seeking Him for the interpretation. The interpretation of dreams or visions is never static.

God is a personal God. Many times He will speak to us in our personal experiences different than He would speak to someone else. For example, my wife Mave was in the restaurant business for twenty years, and I was involved in sports and athletics. Many times God will speak to me in dreams about golf or baseball, but once He spoke to Mave that He was an apple pie, and she was an apple dumpling. The only thing I knew about either one was how to eat them. Mave, on the other hand, knew that all the ingredients in the apple dumpling were also in the apple pie. God was speaking to her that she had everything that was in Him, that she was made in His likeness and image. That revelation spoke wonders to her, but wouldn't have meant much to me.

God knows every place that we have ever been, what we have ever done, every relationship we have ever had, and every voice we have ever heard. It is all recorded in the heart of God in eternity, and He can play it back in a way that we can understand it.

Usually, when God speaks to me symbolically and the natural interpretation doesn't seem to work for me (it's not applicable), then I know that He is prompting me to a deeper place of relationship, and I have to seek Him for the interpretation. I have not because I ask not. And the greater blessing always comes to the seeker.

In 2005, I wrote a book entitled *Night Watch: Unlocking Your Destiny through Dreams and Visions* in which I gave much more detail about dreams and dream interpretation, and in 2018, a revised and updated edition of that book was published. This book could be a great help to you if you have received revelations and don't quite understand how to interpret them. In the book, I included a section on dream symbols that can help you to develop a vocabulary and a dialogue with the Lord. You may order this book from our website: www.eagleworldwide.com or by calling our office at 905-308-9991.

After I have recorded everything I heard God say, I then pray it back to Him and spend time trying to discover exactly what He is wanting to tell me. Our God is a speaking God, and He wants to speak to you and me today!

THE NEEDED WISDOM

The Word of God says: *"Wisdom is the principal thing"* (Proverbs 4:7), and it is indeed the principal thing when it comes to understanding the voice of the Lord. When the Lord speaks to me, I have to know that *He* is doing it and with purpose and design. When I feel that I have heard from God and wish to gain an understanding of the revelation, the first place I need wisdom is in discerning or testing the spirits. Not every voice I hear or every thought I think is from God. The source can be one of the following:

IT CAN BE FROM GOD, BY THE POWER OF THE HOLY SPIRIT

John 14:26

> *But the Comforter, which is the Holy Ghost, whom the Father will send in my name, he shall teach you all things, and bring all things to your remembrance, whatsoever I have said unto you.*

This is the revelation we all seek.

IT CAN BE FROM MAN

The things I hear, however, can come from my own thoughts or emotions, the problems of the day, the concerns and burdens that are on my heart or even from my own desires. Thoughts can be birthed and revelation can come forth, but where is it coming from?

Some people have lots of what we call "pizza dreams." It's not always because they have eaten pizza, but because the revelation is coming from their own thoughts and emotions. I have to get a witness in my spirit. I have to test it by the Spirit. And my spirit must bear witness to it.

Sometimes we can track a thought down to our own flesh or our own soul because it is something we wanted to hear or something we wanted to do. When I receive a revelation that makes me tingly all over, because it is what I wanted, I go out of my way to test it by the Spirit of God and make sure it is backed by His Word.

IT CAN BE FROM SATAN OR DEMONIC SPIRITS

All of us have heard from the demonic realm, and all of us, at times, are susceptible to falling under the influence of those wrong spirits. Luke recorded the fact that Jesus was led by the Spirit of God into the wilderness (see Luke 4:1). There Jesus fasted for forty days and was tempted by the devil (see Luke 4:2). The first voice Jesus heard in verses 3-6 was not the voice of God, but rather the voice of Satan.

Jesus knew what to do in this case. He opposed the tempter with the Word. We need to discern the source of our revelations, know if it is biblical and sound or not. If not, then we must fight Satan with the truth of the Word. If what we are being told is immoral, we can immediately know for a certainty that God is not the source of it.

IT CAN BE FROM AN ANGELIC VISITATION/A THIRD-HEAVEN REVELATION

Throughout the Word of God, God sent angels and brought men of God like Paul to high places in revelation through angelic revelations. But there are angels of light and also angels of darkness, demons representing themselves as being from God.

Joseph Smith, the founder of Mormonism, had what he described as an angelic visitation. But what any angel says has to bear witness with our spirit and has to be backed up by the Word of God. I have read about the encounter Joseph Smith had, and my opinion is this: Moroni was full of baloney.

We must test the spirits and check the source of every revelation, and we must also have the wisdom to know what God wants us to do with each revelation. Does He want us to prophesy? Is He telling us this for our own personal direction? Does He want us to use it for intercession for another person or for the Church as a whole? We need to know what to do with the revelation and its interpretation.

Finally, we need to have wisdom concerning the timing of the fulfillment of the revelation and also the timing for us to act prophetically. We who hear the voice of the Lord must seek Him for the times and the seasons, not just for the mysteries.

The prophet Habakkuk tells us:

Habakkuk 2:3

For the vision is yet for an appointed time, but at the end it shall speak.

We cannot afford to be a moment too soon or a moment too late.

Our God is the God of Abraham, Isaac and Jacob. He is the God of Elijah. He is an on-time God, the show-up God. He showed up for Elijah, and, since He is *"no respecter of persons,"* He will show up for you as well.

We are not the ones who choose the times and the seasons; it is God Himself. He measures time in eternity, whereas man measures it in minutes, hours, days, weeks or months.

Daniel said:

Daniel 2:21-22, My Paraphrase

It is He who changes the times and seasons. It is He who removes and sets up kings. It is He who gives wisdom to the wise and knowledge to them that understand. It is He who reveals the deep secrets. He is the One who reveals the things that are in darkness and brings them to light.

I pray for you the prayer that Paul prayed:

That God may give you revelation and wisdom and understanding, that He would truly guide you and direct you by the power of His Spirit. I pray that the gift of prophecy will be stirred afresh in your heart and that God would put a hunger inside of you to seek Him, to thirst for His presence and His power. I pray that He would raise you up as an end-time warrior, in power and understanding, to do mighty exploits and signs and wonders in His name.

In Jesus' name,
Amen!

Chapter 5

ELEVEN CHANNELS OF PROPHECY

1 Corinthians 14:1, CSB

Pursue love, and desire spiritual gifts, but especially that you may prophesy.

The Bible encourages us to prophesy. But when we do prophesy, we need to know the different ways God operates to deliver the prophetic gift. Prophecy is one of the nine gifts of the Spirit listed in 1 Corinthians 12. In this chapter, I want to discuss eleven channels of prophecy.

The following illustrations from the Word of God give us a template to understand and operate in the fullness of the gift through the eleven channels of prophecy. I believe in the laying on of hands for impartation of the prophetic gifting, and we exercise that in our churches at Eagle Worldwide Ministries. Many times, during worship, the song of the Lord will come forth and, at times, that has been our whole service, as the Holy Spirit has directed.

We are a prophetic church, raising up prophetic people, and you can see the gift of prophecy operating in every service. Personally, I operate in the office of the prophet, and, again, you can see that function flowing in a higher realm because of the anointing to release God's agenda.

As the Church, we all need to allow all eleven channels of prophecy to flow in our lives and in our corporate services, according to God's Word. As we flow in each area and use it more and more, we will be able to see further and hear more clearly what the Lord is saying.

1. The Prophetic Presbytery

1 Timothy 4:14

Neglect not the gift that is in thee, which was given thee by prophecy, with the laying on of the hands of the presbytery.

Acts 13:2-3

As they ministered to the Lord, and fasted, the Holy Ghost said, Separate me Barnabas and Saul for the work whereunto I have called them. And when they had fasted and prayed, and laid their hands on them, they sent them away.

This realm of prophecy is for setting aside those called to the work of the Lord and recognizing and releasing them into their call. It includes: the laying on of hands by men and women of God who meet the qualifications of a presbyter, for the installation of and setting forth into ministry of those who have been proven to be called into ministry leadership; ordination into the five-fold ministry; confirmation and activation of members or ministries and for progress in Christian maturity.

2. Prophetic Evangelism
(Phillip and the eunuch in Acts 8)

The most famous example of this realm of the prophetic is Jesus' unique evangelism of the woman He met at the well in Samaria. God can speak to individuals or groups and gives specific information (i.e. who, what, why, where, when) that will touch them and facilitate a sharing of the Gospel and even leading them to the Lord. This type of prophetic act can impact individuals as well as groups.

Note: Let's not be those who wait. This is always God's will and part of the Great Commission: *"Go ye"* (Matthew 28:19).

3. Prophetic Preaching

1 Peter 4:11

> *If any man speak, let him speak as the oracles of God; if any man minister, let him do it as of the ability which God giveth: that God in all things may be glorified through Jesus Christ, to whom be praise and dominion forever and ever. Amen.*

Have you ever noticed how two people can listen to the same sermon and have completely different comments about how the Lord spoke to them through it? God can use the prophetic preaching of the same message to speak directly into the heart of many individuals exactly what they need to hear. This requires that the preacher not only seeks the Lord for the right word to deliver, but also allows the Lord to speak through him prophetically within the flow of his message.

Prophecy comes by divine inspiration and revelation knowledge, and in the context of a sermon, there may not seem to be any "Thus saith the Lord," but there can be an obvious flow and the prophetic word going forth.

4. The Prophecy of the Scriptures

2 Peter 1:20-21

Knowing this first, that no prophecy of the scripture is of any private interpretation. For the prophecy came not in old time by the will of man: but holy men of God spake as they were moved by the Holy Ghost.

The prophecy of the Scriptures is the only prophecy that can claim infallibility. Right now we are seeing great revelation in end-time prophecy, but we're also seeing the Word of God come alive for the Church to move, mobilize and be equipped. Foundational truths are being restored. All other prophetic utterances are to be judged by the written Word.

5. The Spirit of Prophecy

Revelation 19:10

For the testimony of Jesus is the spirit of prophecy.

The anointing of the Holy Spirit can enable individuals who may not have the gift of prophecy and who are not called to the office of a prophet to speak forth under the inspiration of God. Often, when God uses someone who doesn't ordinarily move in this gift and it is for an appointed situation, that person doesn't usually retain the gift of prophecy. Biblical examples would be King Saul and Balaam. God can use anyone to testify of Jesus!

6. The Office of the Prophet
(See 1 Corinthians 12:28 and Acts 13:1)

The office of the prophet is one of the five-fold ministry gifts listed in Ephesians 4:11, for the equipping of the saints. All who are called to the five-fold office of the prophet have the gift of prophecy, but not all who have the gift of prophecy are five-fold prophets. Those who are called to operate in the office of a prophets are designed to function at a higher realm than those who merely exercise the gift of prophecy.

1 Corinthians 12:28

And God hath set some in the church, first apostles, secondarily prophets, thirdly teachers, after that miracles, then gifts of healings, helps, governments, diversities of tongues.

When someone is operating in the office of a prophet, they begin to flow into the areas of guidance, instruction, rebuke, judgment and revelation. They are especially anointed to perceive what is next on God's agenda for the restoration of the Church and are to send forth a clear sound, revealing God's heart and desire for His Bride and His Army.

Those whom God has called to the office of a prophet often prophesy over regions, leaders, nations or countries and moves of God, and even bring corrective words, as the Old Testament prophets did. Those operating in the gift of prophecy for the edification of the Body and who are not necessarily prophets, will give words that will edify, exhort and encourage. These are two different operations: the office vs. the gift.

7. The Gift of Prophecy
(See 1 Corinthians 12:10, 14:1-4, 6, 22, 24 and 31)

The main function of the gift of prophecy is for the edification, exhortation and comfort of the person or persons to whom it is addressed (sec 1 Corinthians 14:3). Prophecy should edify the Church (see verse 4).

1 Corinthians 12:10

> *To another the working of miracles; to another prophecy; to another discerning of spirits; to another divers kinds of tongues; to another the interpretation of tongues.*

Romans 12:6

> *Having then gifts differing according to the grace that is given to us, whether prophecy, let us prophesy according to the proportion of faith.*

Prophecy is one of the nine signature gifts of the Holy Spirit and is the gift that we often see operating during corporate gatherings for the encouragement and growth of the Body or of individuals, as we speak the word of the Lord to encourage our brothers and sisters.

8. The Song of the Lord

Colossians 3:16

> *Let the word of Christ dwell in you richly in all wisdom; teaching and admonishing one another in psalms and hymns and spiritual songs, singing with grace in your hearts to the Lord.*

With almost every fresh move of God's Spirit, He places an anointing on certain songs and upon certain psalmists who prophesy in song. There is a fresh new anointing in the Body of Christ today for prophetic worship and prophetic releases in song.

9. Prophetic Prayers

Sometimes, during intercession, the person praying will prophetically declare things from the Holy Spirit. This can be an incredibly anointed time of prophetic proclamation.

Jeremiah 27:18

But if they be prophets, and if the word of the LORD be with them, let them now make intercession to the LORD of hosts, that the vessels which are left in the house of the LORD, and in the house of the king of Judah, and at Jerusalem, go not to Babylon.

10. Dreams and Visions

Numbers 12:6

And he said, Hear now my words: If there be a prophet among you, I the LORD will make myself known unto him in a vision, and will speak unto him in a dream.

God longs to speak to His people through dreams and visions today, even as He did in days of old. Ask the Lord to open this incredible realm of hearing and seeing to you!

11. The Visionary Realm

Acts 2:17-18

And it shall come to pass in the last days, saith God, I will pour out of my Spirit upon all flesh: and your sons

*and your daughters shall prophesy, and your young men
shall see visions, and your old men shall dream dreams:
and on my servants and on my handmaidens I will pour
out in those days of my Spirit; and they shall prophesy.*

This visionary realm includes not only seeing the vision
and its direction, but also receiving the mandate that God
is opening up for a church body, a ministry, a people, a
family, an individual or a company. God said that His
people perish without a vision! He wants to open the eyes
of our understanding, so that we can see into the realms
that He has for us. Let's become people of vision—seeing,
believing and walking in the ways the Lord has prepared
for us.

I trust that this teaching has helped you in understanding the various ways that God uses the realms and
channels of prophecy through His servants todays. Again,
I want to recommend my book to you: *Night Watch:
Unlocking Your Destiny through Dreams and Visions.* Many
people have reported that they have received an impartation of prophetic dreams as well as dream interpretation
through reading real-life experiences of how God has
spoken to me to guide me in business, personal decisions
and ministry decision through dreams and visions.

Father, I pray that the eyes of our hearts would be
opened with Your revelation, that we would walk in

all that You have for us, that we would be wise in the prophetic gifting and in the way we reach out to others with this gift.

Father, I thank You that You have chosen to put Your words into our mouths, that we would be used to edify, exhort and comfort men and women, that all would be done in love and that many would come to know You through this gift.

In Jesus' name.

Amen!

Chapter 6

THE MANY GIFTS OF THE SPIRIT AND THEIR USE

1 Corinthians 14:1, NIV

Follow the way of love and eagerly desire gifts of the Spirit, especially the gift of prophecy.

The following teachings on the gifts of the Spirit includes a section where I briefly describe and highlight twenty-six spiritual gifts, broken down into five general categories: (1) The five-fold office gifts, (2) Church leadership gifts, (3) The nine signature gifts of the Holy Spirit, (4) Servanthood gifts and (5) Special gifts. I have included only brief explanations and simple concepts, but I hope that, from this section, you can get an idea about which of these gifts you feel you possess or have been given.

In this chapter, I want to share with you some of the teachings the apostle Paul was led to send to the first-century Church on the gifts of the Spirit at Corinth. These are the most condensed and impactful teachings on the gifts of the Spirit given to us in the Word.

I believe that the Holy Spirit chose Paul to bring this teaching to the Body because, in the New Testament, Paul moved more than anyone else in the operation of these gifts. The saints at Corinth were intelligent, prosperous and gifted, and the Holy Spirit could have chosen to speak about the gifts through Peter or any of the other apostles. Why not James? James sat over the whole council at Jerusalem. He was an apostle to the apostles. Yet the Holy Spirit chose Paul. I believe this was because He knew there was no way the Corinthians (or you and I) could dispute Paul's knowledge, understanding and experience in the gifts because he lived them and flowed in them.

Paul was a man of the Spirit. You can minister in the natural, or you can minister in Spirit. Paul said:

1 Corinthians 2:1-5, NASB

And when I came to you, brethren, I did not come with superiority of speech or of wisdom, proclaiming to you the testimony of God. For I determined to know nothing among you except Jesus Christ, and Him crucified. I was with you in weakness and in fear and in much trembling, and my message and my preaching were not in persuasive words of wisdom, but in demonstration of the Spirit and of power, so that your faith would not rest on the wisdom of men, but on the power of God.

Paul made his choice, and it was to flow in the Spirit. I have made the same choice. How about you?

The verse divisions were added to the Bible by men so that we could find our way around. With Paul, it was all one teaching. In it, he describes the five-fold ministry and the nine signature gifts of the Spirit.

Paul spent all of chapter 13 dealing with the wonderful and powerful gift of love, telling us that if the gifts are not ministered in love, there is only emptiness and hollowness. When ministered in faith and love, there is a depth to the gifts that impacts every person.

Most of chapter 14 of this letter is spent talking about the gift of prophecy. As you may know by now, prophecy is my primary gifting, so I love this fourteenth chapter. Paul opened that chapter with a very powerful directive to you and me:

1 Corinthians 14:1, NIV
Follow the way of love and eagerly desire gifts of the Spirit, especially the gift of prophecy.

Let me remind you again that Paul opened his discussion of spiritual gifts with these powerful words:

1 Corinthians 12:1
Now concerning spiritual gifts, brethren, I would not have you ignorant.

And Paul closed his discussion of spiritual gifts with these equally powerful words:

1 Corinthians 14:40

Let all things be done decently and in order.

Again, I believe it was by divine design that the Holy Spirit chose Paul to bring this very important teaching to the Church. This man had a real personal understanding of the application and operation of spiritual gifts, as he was going out and evangelizing and birthing churches, particularly among the Gentiles. So, let's review a few of the key statements that Paul made in these chapters.

First and foremost, God doesn't want us to be ignorant of these things. Obviously, He wants us to be knowledgeable and to have an understanding of them. And the Lord impressed Paul to deliver them because He wanted us to have his practical understanding.

Early on Paul wrote:

1 Corinthians 12:4

Now there are diversities of gifts, but the same Spirit.

In verses 8-10, Paul went on to list the nine signature gifts of the Holy Spirit. These are ministry gifts that include prophecy, the word of knowledge, the word of wisdom, gifts of healing, the working of miracles, the discernment of spirits and the gifts of tongues and interpretation of tongues, along with the gift of faith.

Most of us have experienced these gifts in operation without love, and we can testify that there was an emptiness, a hollowness, a hardness that was obvious and made what was being offered difficult to receive.

In 1 Corinthians 12:5, Paul said that there are different administrations, but it is the same Lord. I believe that He was letting us understand that when you go from fellowship to fellowship, in different settings, there are different administrations and spiritual oversight, and this requires relationships, recognition of local authority and an understanding of the protocol of the house. This ensures that we will not be disruptive using the gifts, but we will blend in and be supportive of one another. Consequently, we will be doing all things *"decently and in order."*

Paul tells us, in verse 6, that there is a diversity of operations, but it is the same God. This tells us that under the anointing and unction of the Holy Spirit, each of us is able to flow individually and uniquely. Personally, I believe that our God is a God of individuality. He anoints us personally, and He is not a cookie-cutter God. He is a God of creativity, and He wants us to be ourselves, not to be emulating another person. So, just be yourself.

If you have a desire to operate in the gifts of the Spirit and know that you are called to minister in the Spirit, you should study the rest of Paul's teachings to the Corinthians concerning spiritual gifts (1 Corinthians 12:1-14:4) in an easy-to-read-and-understand version of the Bible.

Now here is that list of the spiritual gifts, with a brief and simple definition, broken down into the five mentioned categories. Read through them and try to identify those that you feel

God has activated in your own life because this word, *"concerning spiritual gifts, brethren, I would not have you ignorant,"* is for you.

As you read, may the Lord richly bless you and stir within you afresh the gifts and the power of His Spirit, and may there be an impartation and an understanding that will allow you to demonstrate and manifest His love.

THE FIVE-FOLD OFFICE GIFTS

Ephesians 4:11-12

And he gave some, apostles; and some, prophets; and some, evangelists; and some, pastors and teachers; for the perfecting of the saints, for the work of the ministry, for the edifying of the body of Christ.

APOSTLES

The office gift of apostle is when God gives special ability and talent to a certain individual in the Body of Christ, to assume and exercise general leadership over a number of churches, ministries or a denomination. This is one of the foundational gifts described in Ephesians 2:20. Many times an apostle is given power and authority to plant, establish and build churches and generally oversee works and the other leaders need. An example is a pastor to pastors.

PROPHETS

This office gift is also under the foundational ministries for building, directing and developing churches and leaders.

A prophet will often have an extraordinarily powerful gift of prophecy, and people will sense that their utterances are divinely-anointed and confirm other prophetic words that are spoken. Prophets are gifted to receive and communicate the word, the message and direction of the Lord to His Body. Many times they will be called upon to raise up other prophetic voices and will teach and preach with great revelation knowledge and insight from the Word of God.

EVANGELISTS

All of us in the Body are called to win souls, but an evangelist is an individual who holds an office in the Church and has an extraordinary hunger for souls. Often, this individual will be involved in developing outreach programs that help others to participate in soul-winning endeavors. Evangelists have a great passion to preach God's Word of salvation. Usually they themselves have a great fear of the Lord, and the anointing on their lives will draw people in large numbers to hear the truth proclaimed—publicly and privately.

TEACHERS

The gift of teaching is the special ability that God gives to certain members of the Body of Christ to communicate information relevant to the health and ministry of the Body and its members in such a way that others will easily and quickly learn. This individual is described by the Scriptures as *"apt to teach"* (1 Timothy 3:2 and 2 Timothy 2:24).

PASTORS

The gift of pastor is the special ability that God gives to certain members of the Body of Christ to assume a long-term personal responsibility for the spiritual welfare of a group of believers. A pastor will clearly have the heart of a shepherd. They will care for the people the Lord has placed in their case in a very personal way, many times becoming involved in their spiritual growth, counseling, bringing guidance, comfort and strength in times of personal hardship, and exhorting them in their personal life to reach their God-given goals and utilize their gifts.

In larger church settings, a pastor will develop a care team to work with individuals. Some of their duties will include home and hospital visitation and organizing and structuring church services and other programs at the local church level.

LEADERSHIP GIFTS

In the biblical structure for the Church, given to us by the apostle Paul, he spoke specifically of three leadership categories: (1) Bishops, (2) Deacons and (3) Elders.

BISHOPS
(SEE 1 TIMOTHY 3:1-7)

The office of bishop can be described as a spiritual overseer of one or more churches or ministries. Many times a bishop will not only oversee and pastor the pastors, but will also preside over special services and events relating to the spiritual network that he or she oversees. Often, in a network of ministries, the bishop will sit on the board of presbyters that certifies, credentials or ordains ministers.

DEACONS

Paul taught about deacons in 1 Timothy 3:8-13 (mainly detailing their required character qualities). In Acts 6, the original apostles selected seven deacons (which included Stephen and Philip), to do the daily work of ministry. The position of deacon is, many times, a practical ministry experience.

Acts 6 speaks of deacons serving, waiting on tables and meeting the needs of widows. Shortly after that, in Acts 7, we see where Stephen went out and began to preach, confronted false spiritual leaders of the time and, eventually, became the first Christian martyr. In Acts 8, Philip began to evangelize, bringing a great move of the Spirit to the city of Samaria, moving in signs, wonders and miracles and preaching with great power.

Deacons may also participate in baptisms, as Philip did with the Ethiopian eunuch. In Acts 21, this same Philip, along with his four daughters, who were prophetic, hosted Paul and his entire company in Caesarea, again utilizing his gift of hospitality.

ELDERS

Paul described elders in 1 Timothy 5:17-22. Some of them will be five-fold ministers, some will have rule and authority over others, and some will labor in the Word and in doctrine. Paul also tells us that elders are laborers worthy of their reward and should not be accused lightly or without multiple confirmations. Peter addressed the first chapter of his first letter to elders and considered himself to be an elder. He exhorted other elders to feed the flock, to provide oversight, to be Christian examples and shepherds in submission to the Chief Shepherd.

THE NINE SIGNATURE GIFTS OF THE HOLY SPIRIT
(Ministry Gifts)

These gifts are outlined in Paul's teachings beginning in 1 Corinthians 12:1, where he states, as we have seen, *"Now concerning spiritual gifts brethren, I would not have you ignorant"* and he completes his teaching on the gifts and their operation in 1 Corinthians 14:40, where he exhorts us to utilize these gifts *"decently and in order."*

The gifts of the Holy Spirit are available to all believers, to be used for the edification of the Body, and are not restricted in any way to those who hold a leadership role or office.

THE REVELATORY GIFTS

PROPHECY

With the gift of prophecy, God drops a message into the heart of an individual, allowing him to receive and communicate this message to others individually or to the Body of Christ at large, or, at times over cities or nations. Not everyone who has the gift of prophecy is in the office of a prophet, but every prophet will have a very special gift of prophecy.

The New Testament model for prophecy is found in 1 Corinthians 14:3, which shows that these gift are to be used to exhort, encourage and edify.

THE WORD OF KNOWLEDGE

With this gift, God sovereignly drops into the spirit of a believer a word of knowledge, or information, not previously known to the individual in the natural. This information will allow them to bring counsel, direction or divine insight that will have a special effect on the person receiving the information. As an example, when the Lord ministered to the woman at the well about her personal relationships, what He knew about her brought her to repentance and the acknowledgment that He was from God.

THE WORD OF WISDOM

With this gift, God sovereignly drops into the spirit of a believer divine wisdom that will help them minister, give counsel or direction to another believer or to the entire Body of Christ. Sometimes a word of wisdom can be dropped into the spirit of a believer to be used to preach or teach, bringing guidance, direction or change to the Body. In the same encounter with the woman at the well, Jesus gave her a bit of wisdom, that God was looking for worshipers who would worship Him in Spirit and in truth.

THE DISCERNING OF SPIRITS

The gift of discerning of spirits is the special ability that God gives to certain members of the Body of Christ to know with assurance whether certain behavior purported to be of God is, in reality, divine, or if it might be human or even satanic.

SPEAKING IN TONGUES

The gift of tongues is the special ability that God gives to certain members of the Body of Christ (a) to speak to God in a language they have never learned and/or (b) to receive and communicate an immediate message from God to His people through a divinely-anointed utterance given in a language they have never learned. It, therefore, requires interpretation.

THE INTERPRETATION OF TONGUES

This gift is the special ability God gives to certain members of the Body of Christ to make known in the vernacular the message given one who speaks in tongues.

THE POWER GIFTS

FAITH

The gift of faith is the special ability that God gives to certain members of the Body of Christ to discern with extraordinary confidence the will and purposes of God for His work.

THE WORKING OF MIRACLES

The gift of miracles is the special ability that God gives to certain members of the Body of Christ to serve as human intermediaries through whom it pleases Him to perform powerful acts that are perceived by observers to have altered the ordinary course of nature.

GIFTS OF HEALING

The gifts of healing are special abilities that God gives to certain members of the Body of Christ to serve as human intermediaries through whom it pleases Him to cure illness and restore health apart from the use of natural means.

SERVANTHOOD GIFTS

These categories of gifts are given to individuals who play a strong supporting role in ministering to the Body, mainly in church and para-church ministries. Many times these gifts are used to support the pastoral work of the church in a practical ministry application.

EXHORTATION

The gift of exhortation is the special ability God gives to certain members of the Body of Christ to minister words of comfort, consolation, encouragement and counsel to other members of the Body in such a way that they feel helped and healed.

GIVING

The gift of giving is the special ability God gives to certain members of the Body of Christ to contribute their material resources to the work of the Lord with liberality and cheerfulness.

HELPS

The gift of helps is the special ability God gives to certain members of the Body of Christ to invest the talents they have in the life and ministry of other members of the Body, thus enabling others to increase the effectiveness of their own spiritual gifts.

MERCY

The gift of mercy is the special ability God gives to certain members of the Body of Christ to feel genuine empathy and compassion for individuals (both Christian and non-Christian) who suffer distressing physical, mental or emotional problems and to translate that compassion into cheerfully-done deeds which reflect Christ's love and alleviate the suffering.

HOSPITALITY

The gift of hospitality is the special ability God gives to certain members of the Body of Christ to provide an open house and a warm welcome to those in need of food and lodging.

LEADERSHIP

The gift of leadership is the special ability God gives to certain members of the Body of Christ to set goals in accordance with God's purpose for the future and to communicate these goals in such a way that their followers voluntarily and harmoniously work together to accomplish them.

INTERCESSION

The gift of intercession is the special ability God gives to certain members of the Body of Christ to pray for extended periods of time on a regular basis and see frequent and specific answers to their prayers, to a degree much greater than that which is expected of the average Christian.

SERVICE

The gift of service is the special ability God gives to certain members of the Body of Christ to identify the unmet needs involved in a task related to God's work and to make use of available resources to meet those needs and help accomplish the desired results.

ADMINISTRATION

The gift of administration is the special ability God gives to certain members of the Body of Christ to understand clearly the immediate and long-range goals of a particular unit of the Body of Christ and to devise and execute effective plans for the accomplishment of those goals.

SPECIAL GIFTS

CELIBACY

The gift of celibacy is the special ability God gives to certain members of the Body of Christ to remain single and enjoy it, to be unmarried and not suffer undue sexual temptation. Sometimes, by the grace of God, we can receive this gift on a temporary basis while awaiting our God-given mate. The Word of God clearly tells us that no one should be forbidden to marry, but some are called by God and ordained to remain so. This should never be a human choice, but, rather, in response to a call by God.

MARTYRDOM

The gift of martyrdom is the special ability God gives to certain members of the Body of Christ to undergo suffering for the faith, even to the point of death, while consistently displaying a joyous and victorious attitude which brings glory to God.

LOVE

The gift of love is the special ability God gives to certain members of the Body of Christ to extend love. We are all to love, but these individuals have a special love.

Now, before we finish this chapter, I would like to pray for you for impartation of spiritual gifts. Paul wrote to the Roman believers:

Romans 1:11-12

For I long to see you, that I may impart to you some spiritual gift, to the end that ye may be established; that is, that I may be comforted together with you by the mutual faith both of you and me.

Right now, let's you and I put our faith together and believe for an impartation of spiritual gifts, that the Father would establish you in your ministry gifting and calling.

Heavenly Father, I come to You now in the name of Jesus Christ, the Giver of all gifts, and in the power of the Holy Spirit. I thank You for an impartation, for an empowerment, for an enduement from Heaven for my brothers and sisters, that You would stir afresh in them all the gifts and all the power of the Holy Spirit.

In Jesus' name,
Amen!

Chapter 7

PROPHETIC STREAMS

1 Peter 2:9

But ye are a chosen generation, a royal priesthood, an holy nation, a peculiar people; that ye should shew forth the praises of him who hath called you out of darkness into his marvellous light.

We are entering one of the most exciting times the earth has ever seen, the raising of an end-time army, an army that is emerging globally as a distinct nation. The Bible calls it *"an holy nation."* This is a nation whose weapons of warfare will not be turned against flesh and blood, but will be utilized to the pulling down of strongholds.

This is an army of people who know their God and His ways, a people who are stepping up and stepping out, a people hearing the heartbeat of their Father and allowing Him to equip them and get them ready, ready to take back what the enemy has stolen, ready to plunder the marketplace and the mountains of the world, a people who will walk in unity as we walk in one Spirit—the Holy Spirit.

In this chapter, I want to make you aware of how the different streams of the anointing in the Spirit working in the hearts of God's people are to flow when we move in His wisdom and strategy. Globally, we are getting ready for a great harvest. The prophetic anointing is calling forth those things that are not as though they were, as we speak forth what we hear the Father saying. I believe that this end-time prophetic army will flow in many anointings, and many varied prophetic streams are now beginning to flow together.

These are the days of Elijah, and these are the days of the harvest! The harvest is here, and the harvest is now! Everywhere I look, everywhere I turn and everywhere I go, the fields are white and ready for harvest.

God's end-time army is to have the anointing of Elijah, to prepare the way of the Lord, make bold proclamations, declaring the Kingdom of God and confronting sin and the enemy. This was the anointing that was on John the Baptist when He prepared the way for the ministry of Jesus.

In the summer of 2000, I was in Ashland, Virginia at Calvary Pentecostal Camp and during worship one day I received a vision of the map of North America. It looked like a weather map. In my vision, streams and rivers secmed to all be flowing toward the center, into a big river going right down the middle of the map.

Then the scene changed, and I was looking at a corn field, and Jesus walked out of the corn field. He was walking in water up to His ankles. I looked at His hands and His feet, and there were no scars.

Then I saw young people. First there were five, then ten, then twenty and they were coming out of the corn field behind Jesus. Then the Lord spoke to me and said, "When the different streams of the anointing, the different streams of the Spirit and the hearts of my people, begin to flow together, know that there will be a great move of the Spirit throughout North America. It will travel right through the heartland."

I asked the Lord, "Why didn't You have any scars on Your hands and feet?"

He said, "When My Body (made up of My people) comes out for the harvest, they will come forth healed and whole."

The Lord told me there would be a great harvest among the youth, and I believe we are moving quickly into that season. When we begin to flow in unity, different streams flowing together, that is the prelude to the harvest.

I'm not just talking about the prophetic anointing of Elijah. I am also referring to the anointing of Joshua, to cross over and occupy the land. I'm talking about the anointing of John the Revelator. He had the greatest revelation of Jesus ever recorded. He was Jesus' friend, and on the night when Jesus was betrayed, John laid his head upon the bosom of the Lord, wanting to hear His heartbeat.

This is the generation that will seek the Lord's heart, not His hand. Their heartcry will be worship and intimacy.

Right now, I believe the prophetic anointing being released to the Church today is the anointing that was on the sons of Issachar:

1 Chronicles 12:32

And the children of Issachar, which were men that had understanding of the times, to know what Israel ought to do; the heads of them were two hundred; and all their brethren were at their commandment.

That is what we need, not just vision, but strategy to know the heart and the timing of God for our generation This is the end-time generation, made up of end-time warriors and end-time handmaidens properly prepared and positioned. Like the army of Joel, they will be climbing the walls. Mighty men, they will understanding spiritual authority and not break rank. They will conquer real life issues, impacting their cities and nations. These will be men and women who live by faith, hearing God's voice and being led by His Spirit. These are the sons and daughters of God.

Let us, you and I, begin at once to seek Him for the higher, for the deeper, for the surer word. This word will not only tell us what God wants, but also what He wants us to do and how He wants us to do it. His vision will provide the necessary strategy. Let's seek Him for an action plan.

You and I ... we are the children of the harvest, and these are the days of harvest. Jesus is the Lord of the harvest, and He is in covenant with our seed. The Bible calls it a *"perpetual covenant"* (see Genesis 9:12, Exodus 31:16 and Jeremiah 50:5). God's heart is for the harvest That's what He is all about. Let Him position you right now and give you His plan for your part the that mighty harvest.

May the Lord richly bless you with revelation, wisdom and understanding. May the prophetic anointing on your life increase. May He grant you a hunger in your heart to seek Him.

May He give us a heart that longs for Him. May He give us a heart for souls, a heart for the harvest, a heart after His own heart, like the heart of David, a heart quick to go to worship and a heart quick to go to war, because the Lord of Hosts is the Lord of the Harvest. You said, in Exodus 15:3, "The Lord is a man of war: the Lord is His name." We join Him in the battle.

In Jesus' name,
Amen!

Chapter 8

A NEW DIMENSION OF KINGDOM REVELATION

Ephesians 1:4-5, NKJV

Just as He chose us in Him before the foundation of the world, that we should be holy and without blame before Him in love, having predestined us to adoption as sons by Jesus Christ to Himself, according to the good pleasure of His will.

As you and I release Jesus' ministry in the earth, our faith must be built upon the rock of revelation. God reveals Himself personally to each of us, imparting that dimension of revelation, that Jesus is the Son of God. He alone imparts the revelation of Who He is. Intimacy with the Spirit of God and dwelling in His presence is key.

God chose us before the beginning of time. Once we receive the revelation of Who He is in us and who we are in Him, our lives are never the same. We can then begin to focus on God's purposes.

In this chapter, I will be focusing on the importance of knowing that our Father wants to reveal Himself to us.

He does this for His glory and because of His love that abounds toward us. Yes, these are days of revelation glory, revelation that brings us into the fullness of the Kingdom dimension.

Ephesians 3:19-20
> *And to know the love of Christ, which passeth knowledge, that ye might be filled with all the fulness of God. Now unto him that is able to do exceeding abundantly above all that we ask or think, according to the power that worketh in us ...*

Things first happen on the inside of us before they happen on the outside. It is the power of Christ working within that produces an outward result. The outer world, therefore, always matches the inner world. Our world is never bigger on the outside than it is on the inside.

The Lord said that the Kingdom of God is within. *"For as* [a man] *thinks in his heart, so is he"* (Proverbs 23:7, NKJV). Who is this Christ and what are you going to do with Him? He is Christ, the hope of Glory within you.

While He was on the earth, the Lord spoke in parables and allegories and ministered with questions. Think about that. Jesus, the One who had all the answers, ministered in questions.

Western culture tends to teach through lecture. Eastern culture, especially Middle-Eastern culture, has a deeper method of learning that challenges a man with questions, so that he must bring forth revelation within his own thoughts and through his own tongue. And that is the way Jesus ministered. His questions did not always make sense to those who heard Him, and they were also not able to discern His motives. His thoughts are not our thoughts, and His ways are not our ways (see Isaiah 55:8).

When God teaches you, it is a process of drawing truth out of you from the inside. The Kingdom of God is big in you! It is SO big in you!

Jesus asked a blind man, *"What do you want?"* He knew what the blind man wanted. But He also knew that the blind man needed to hear from his own mouth the issue of his heart and to declare it, by his faith, so that Christ could do what he wanted and needed.

In Matthew 16, we see Jesus asking questions of His disciples:

Matthew 16:13-18

When Jesus came into the coasts of Caesarea Philippi, he asked his disciples, saying, Whom do men say that I the Son of man am?

And they said, Some say that thou art John the Baptist: some, Elias; and others, Jeremias, or one of the prophets.

He saith unto them, But whom say ye that I am?

And Simon Peter answered and said, Thou art the Christ, the Son of the living God.

And Jesus answered and said unto him, Blessed art thou, Simon Bar-Jona: for flesh and blood hath not revealed it unto thee, but my Father which is in heaven. And I say also unto thee, That thou art Peter, and upon this rock I will build my church; and the gates of hell shall not prevail against it.

Certainly it was important to Jesus to know who other people thought He was. But the important thing to the disciples was who *they* thought He was. In order for a revelation to be effective in the life of any believer, it must become personal. Who is Christ to you?

Christ is not Jesus' last name. It is who He was. Peter declared it after he heard it from God. Jesus will never be bigger and never more than you and I declare Him to be in our own lives.

Paul taught the Roman believers:

Romans 10:9-10

That if thou shalt confess with thy mouth the Lord Jesus, and shalt believe in thine heart that God hath raised him from the dead, thou shalt be saved. For with the heart man believeth unto righteousness; and with the mouth confession is made unto salvation.

What I receive is always according to my declaration. Let's begin to make bold proclamations, declaring the Kingdom of God! Let's call those things that are not, *"as though they were"* (Romans 4:17). Let's command our morning at the start of each day (see Job

38:12). This is not just about speaking. Truly believing in my heart what I speak ... that is faith!

Real revelation can be shared by man, but it is given by the Spirit. Jesus said that He would build His Church *"upon this rock"* (Matthew 16:18). His Church is the Kingdom revelation of His people. He didn't build the Church upon Peter, the little stone, but upon the solid rock of revelation. And the Kingdom in you will be built upon revelation too. When you have a revelation from Heaven, that is when *"the gates of Hell shall not prevail against it."*

Revelation is not hidden *from* us. It is something that is hidden *for* us. Jesus said to His Father in prayer, *"Thou hast hid these things from the wise and prudent, and hast revealed them unto babes"* (Matthew 11:25). That doesn't mean He wants us to act like children, but, rather, that He wants us to be dependent upon Him. When we get revelation, there comes a responsibility to receive it, believe it and obey it.

Jesus said:

John 15:16

Ye have not chosen me, but I have chosen you, and ordained you, that ye should go and bring forth fruit, and that your fruit should remain: that whatsoever ye shall ask of the Father in my name, he may give it you.

Revelation glory is God continuing to try and reveal Himself to us. That revelation is for you and for me. He *wants* to reveal Himself to us.

Deuteronomy 29:29

The secret things belong unto the LORD our God: but those things which are revealed belong unto us and to our children for ever, that we may do all the words of this law.

So, the secret things belong to the Lord, but those things which are revealed belong to us, to His children, forever. Look deeper. He has more for you, more than you can imagine. Only believe. Seek, knock and ask, and you will surely find!

Jesus said:

Luke 12:32

Fear not, little flock; for it is your Father's good pleasure to give you the kingdom.

Look what it says in the book of Acts:

Acts 19:11-20, MSG

God did powerful things through Paul, things quite out of the ordinary. The word got around and people started taking pieces of clothing—handkerchiefs and scarves and the like— that had touched Paul's skin and then touching the sick with them. The touch did it—they were healed and whole.

Some itinerant Jewish exorcists who happened to be in town at the time tried their hand at what they assumed to be Paul's "game." They pronounced the name of the Master Jesus over victims of evil spirits, saying, "I command you by the Jesus preached by Paul!" The seven sons of a certain Sceva, a Jewish high priest, were trying to do this on a man when the evil spirit talked back: "I know Jesus and I've heard of Paul, but who are you?" Then the possessed man went berserk—jumped the exorcists, beat them up, and tore off their clothes. Naked and bloody, they got away as best they could.

It was soon news all over Ephesus among both Jews and Greeks. The realization spread that God was in and behind this. Curiosity about Paul developed into reverence for the Master Jesus. Many of those who thus believed came out of the closet and made a clean break with their secret sorceries. All kinds of witches and warlocks came out of the woodwork with their books of spells and incantations and made a huge bonfire of them. Someone estimated their worth at fifty thousand silver coins. In such ways it became evident that the Word of the Master was now sovereign and prevailed in Ephesus.

"So the Word of the Lord grew mightily and prevailed."

That's what we need today, for these are perilous times, just as Paul described in 2 Timothy 3:1-7. And drastic times require drastic measures. So let's be radical Christians, making radical choices and radical commitments!

Living on the Prophetic Edge

Father, You are mighty! Your love for us is immeasurable. I pray for Kingdom revelation to come upon all Your people, that they would rise up in all the fullness of the knowledge and glory of all that You are and all that You would be in us and through us. Father, I pray that our lives would be revolutionized and we would rise up as warriors in Your Word and in Your Spirit, living radical lives for Your glory.

In Jesus' name,
Amen!

Chapter 9

THE SONG OF THE LORD

Isaiah 42:9-10, KJ21

Behold, the former things are come to pass, and new things do I declare: before they spring forth I tell you of them. Sing unto the LORD a new song, and his praise from the end of the earth, ye that go down to the sea, and all that is therein; the isles, and the inhabitants thereof.

More and more, we are beginning to hear the song of the Lord in our gatherings. This us not just true at Eagle Worldwide Ministries, but at ministries around the world. In this chapter, I will focus on this important prophetic phenomenon.

What is the song of the Lord? It is a supernatural song, spontaneously coming forth from the Spirit of God. The song of the Lord is expressed as a prophetic song, and it brings encouragement, exhortation and comfort.

Although some people will have a ministry of singing the song of the Lord, others may also minister the song of the Lord at various times. We are seeing an emergence of the song of the Lord with great worshipers, such as my wife, Mave Moyer, Joanne McFatter, Julie Myers and many others. It is truly a beautiful gifting in which the Bridegroom sings to His Bride.

In every move of the Spirit, it seems, the Lord anoints the worship in a special way, putting His finger on a particular song or style, almost as if that music was ordained *"for such a time as this."* We know that the Lord is *"the same yesterday, today and forever,"* but I say to you: He is singing a new song. He is releasing a new sound.

Isaiah foretold a new thing springing forth in a dry place, a refreshing, a revival of the heart of worship and the heart of the worshiper. This is it.

When I speak about the song of the Lord, I am not necessarily referring to this new music that is being released. I am specifically speaking of the spontaneous, prophetic song that the Lord ordains in the heart of worship. You hear talk of it occurring at Azusa Street, during the Welsh Revival and at other places where the Lord moved in power in the heart of the worshipers.

The place I personally saw this gift in operation more than anywhere else was in the life and ministry of Ruth Heflin, Jane Lowder and so many others at Calvary Campground in Ashland, Virginia and at their Mount Zion Fellowship in Jerusalem. Their revelation of the glory, their heart to worship, their prophetic mantle and their openness to hear the voice of the

Lord has made Calvary one of the real forerunner ministries in ushering in the glory realm and the song of the Lord.

As I noted, my wife, Mave, also has that same anointing. The way the Spirit operates in and through her is very poetic, as well as prophetic (see the following chapter). When I first met Mave in Canada in 2000, during a particular service she would receive wonderful poems and/or song that conveyed the exact message the Lord had laid on my heart to preach that night. She often told me that she had felt, in some way, divinely inspired, but I told her I believed it was deeper than that. I was convinced that what was happening with Mave was the administration and operation of her prophetic gift, according to 1 Corinthians 12.

This was the same gift, from the same Lord and same Spirit, just a different and unique operation through her than through others. I also told her that I felt it was one of the eleven biblical channels and realms of prophecy that I had seen in the Word of God.

In Colossians, Paul taught:

Colossians 3:16

Let the word of Christ dwell in you richly in all wisdom; teaching and admonishing one another in psalms and hymns and spiritual songs, singing with grace in your hearts to the Lord.

This should be the natural prophetic overflow of a heart

filled with the love of God.

Mave's teaching on this subject is not only informative and powerful; she also has the ability and anointing to impart this gift to others.

The Scriptures teach that the ministry of music is to be a two-way conversation between the Lord and His redeemed. We are to speak to ourselves and to one another *"in songs and hymns and spiritual songs,"* and to Jesus. This must not be a one-sided conversation.

During our services, given the opportunity, the Lord Jesus will speak to us through worship. When this occurs, the prophetic word, or song, will usually line up with the preaching of the Word and confirm it. In the spiritual ministry of worship, there is a deep flow of the anointing to break bondages and save souls. This type of flow will only come forth if we yield to God's Spirit and understand the truth of His Word concerning the spiritual songs of the Lord.

The song of the Lord is the ministry of the heart. It is a spiritual song, fresh and new, hot off the heavenly press. Because of this, not everyone likes this song. It can irritate the flesh of those who have no relationship or intimacy with the Lord, but it will always bring those who do into a closer, more cherished place with the Lord.

Every man and women is born with a great musical instrument—their voice. We can use our voices, in words and song, to praise and worship God our Creator, to express love or concern for others, to speak to the Lord, to exhort, encourage and edify the Body of Christ. Music is just another form this communication.

God formed us with vocal chords and a windpipe. The upper part of the windpipe contains the vocal cords. Do you know what goes through that pipe? The wind, or breath, of the Holy Spirit, and as that wind blows across the strings of our hearts, and it causes us to sing the rhythms of eternity.

The Scriptures tell us much about this beautiful song of the Lord. Many times we are told, throughout the Bible, that we will sing a *"new song."* Many of the songs we sing are praises or adorations unto God. There is a difference between merely singing and praising and singing the song of the Lord. When we are praising God, we are worshiping Him. When we are singing the song of the Lord, we are revealing Jesus Christ. When we are living and walking in Him, and He is our All in All, we can sing this *"new song."*

To sing any natural song, we need to know the words and the melody, but since the new song comes straight from Heaven above (no man writes it; it is divinely inspired), as we sing and follow the flow of the Spirit, it is much like a river winding and taking us to places that are new and exciting. A river never flows straight to its destination. It takes many twists and turns on its journey. As we follow the river of God, we will flow much like a natural river, sensing His changing flow and His refreshing and responding to it. Sometimes the flow will take us through calm waters, but sometimes we will pass through a series of rapids and churned-up waters. Why? Because God is never predictable. The song of the Lord or the prophetic word that comes forth will come in His way, sometimes gentle and peaceful and sometimes not! Just flow with it!

Moses sang:

Exodus 15:2

The Lord is my strength and song, and he is become my salvation: he is my God, and I will prepare him a habitation; my father's God, and I will exalt him.

The psalmist David sang:

Psalm 118:14

The Lord is my strength and song, and is become my salvation.

Isaiah sang:

Isaiah 12:2

Behold, God is my salvation; I will trust, and not be afraid: for the Lord Jehovah is my song.

By doing God's will, which is sharing what the Lord is showing us, and by simply manifesting Him in our lives, we are singing His song and walking in His Word.

Remember: the truth of the Word in our lives is the action it takes. Faith without works is dead and will never produce for the Kingdom of God. We can talk and we can sing, but if we can't walk the walk, we're not doing a thing!

Again, it was David who sang:

Psalm 28:7

The LORD is my strength and my shield; my heart trusted in him, and I am helped; therefore my heart greatly rejoices; and with my song will I praise him.

The new song is the testimony of Jesus Christ, and it has the power and force to set creation free. We are privileged to be the singers. The song that we sing is a new song—the living word of God.

How do you know you are hearing God. Here are some keys to help you discern it.

SOME KEYS TO HEARING GOD:

Key #1 – God's voice in our heart sounds like a flow of spontaneous thoughts. Therefore, when I tune to God, I tune to spontaneity.

Key #2 – Keep your thought life pure and stay away from vain imaginations. An unsanctified imagination brings perverted revelation.

Key #3 – I must learn to still my own thoughts and emotions so that I can sense God's flow of thoughts and emotions within me.

Mave and I come together in agreement right now with you, and we know that God confirms His word. We both believe strongly in the power of impartation, and we believe for you. Join your faith together with ours as we pray.

Heavenly Father, we come to You in the Name of Jesus Christ, the Giver of the gifts, and in power of the Holy Spirit. We know, Lord, that we can receive impartation and gifting by putting our faith together, by the laying on of hands and by prophetic declaration. I thank You that my brothers and sisters are receiving right now an impartation of the gift of prophecy, the song of the Lord. May the Spirit of the living God and the prophetic anointing begin to well up within them.

Thank You that they will receive dreams and visions, revelations from the heavenlies and that You are anointing their hearts and their voices with the sounds of Glory and the song of the Lord. Let it bubble up within them ... until it flows like a beautiful prophetic river.

In Jesus' glorious name,
Amen!

Chapter 10

POETIC PROPHECY

Colossians 3:16

Let the word of Christ dwell in you richly in all wisdom; teaching and admonishing one another in psalms and hymns and spiritual songs, singing with grace in your hearts to the Lord.

As I mentioned in the previous chapter, my wife, Mave, has a wonderful gifting in the prophetic. She didn't even realize she had such a beautiful gift until she started receiving downloads of poetry from the Holy Spirit. Eventually she started singing the poetry, and it quickly transformed into prophetic songs from the Lord. When I listen to her sing these inspired songs, I find it to be one of the most beautiful ways I hear God speak.

In this chapter, Mave will share her experiences in this area. Before we get to that, let me encourage you to always carry some paper and a pen with you. Then, when you are in the midst of corporate worship or even when you are by yourself and you enter a place of praise and worship, you can write down what you are hearing in the Spirit.

Do you think that you don't have a spiritual gift? Do you understand the way a gift operates in the life of a believer? The gifts of God are in operation even when we don't realize it. The apostle Paul said this:

> *Now concerning spiritual gifts, brethren, I would not have you ignorant* [or without knowledge of what they are and how they operate]. 1 Corinthians 12:1

Now to Mave's portion:

In the fall of 2000, Dr. Russ Moyer came to Canada with a revelation of the prophetic and apostolic ministry I had never heard before. He was preaching five-fold ministry and the priesthood of the believer and how we were all called to the ministry of Jesus Christ. He was teaching on the gifts of the Spirit and how we all had at least one gift, but that we could function in more than one gift as the Spirit of God willed. This was an exciting time for all of us, as we began to experience the power of God in our own lives, moving through us in ways we had never known before.

I was part of a team of people who gathered around Russ in this season, and we were equipped and began moving in ministry gifts. We then began traveling out with him to other places and praying for the sick, prophesying, operating in the word of knowledge and wisdom, admonishing and encouraging the Body of believers. It was exhilarating to move in and experience the Spirit of God in such a new and unusual way.

During this time, I would get what I thought was a divinely-inspired poem. It would come very quickly and unexpectedly, and I had to write it down or I would forget and lose what I was hearing. Something similar had begun happening to me from time to time when I was attending Bible school in Oklahoma, but now it was an every-service occurrence.

Dr. Russ began to teach that God works His gifts in all of us in ways that are suited to our personality and character. He explained that God uses people, places and things that we are familiar with to communicate to us. I began to understand that this poetic expression was actually a prophetic word from the Lord, a poetic prophecy like Paul spoke of in Colossians 3:16:

Let the word of Christ dwell in you richly as you sing psalms, hymns and spiritual songs with gratitude in your hearts to God.   (My paraphrase)

As I began to understand this gift and how it worked in me, it very quickly became a spiritual song, and I was able to move in the ministry of the psalmist.

In all of this, I realized just how much of a personal God He was and how much He loved me and wanted to communicate with me in a way that I could understand. There is such a freedom in knowing that God is still speaking to His children today. He really is *"the same, yesterday, and today and forever."*

Now, when I have these experiences, I know that the Lord wants me to release these words over the Body of Christ. Sometimes I will move in prophetic song and sing a word over some individual, and, at times, I have brought an entire message in song.

The Spirit of God is always flowing, always moving, always bringing life. He is a God of individuality, and He wants to work with us in a way that we understand and comprehend. He is a mystery, but He longs to identify with you and me.

When we can grasp the truth that God wants us to hear His voice for ourselves and that He wants us to know the times and the seasons, our lives become more exciting and fulfilling in serving Him. There is no greater experience than hearing from the Lord and walking in His ways.

This truly is a new day, a day of understanding and change, a day in which many of the things we have believed for are coming to pass, a day that our faith is becoming sight!

Here are a couple of examples of prophetic poems the Lord has given me:

THE ABC'S OF FAITH

Faith is a persuasion,
The thing that you believe,

A steadfastly set conviction
From which you will not leave.

To obtain it, you must hear the Word
And accept that it is true.
Then you will see how quickly
Faith will come to you.

Faith must be released now
Or it is lifeless, dead, alone.
So, with the fruit of your own lips,
Make your beliefs be known.

Faith alone is useless;
With works, it is complete.
Hook your mouth up with your heart,
For faith that can't be beat.

Continue now to feed your faith
In all areas with God's Word.
Putting on the breastplate of righteousness,
With truth, our loins we gird.

Faith must be the leader.
We must respect his ways.
By asking him the questions,
Can I think, and do and say?

Yes, faith must be the leader.
We follow close at hand.
Then we can walk in victory
Into the Promised Land.

If flesh becomes the ruler,
The senses say ... "Retreat!"
Faith becomes abandoned,
And we walk in defeat.

So, feed upon the Scriptures.
Hook your mouth up to your heart.
You pick up the shield of faith
And quench the fiery darts.

Now, faith has been established.
Of God's promise we're assured.
If we mix equal parts of patience,
Stand steadfast and endure.

After all that we have studied,
And after all that we've been through,
We endeavor not to hear alone ...
But step out in faith and DO.

This poetic prophetic word was given to me during my faith class at
Rhema Bible School in Tulsa, Oklahoma. I framed it and gave it to
my teacher, Doug Jones, January 1996.

A PLACE CALLED GRACE

Grace is a position,
The place in which we stand,
Where we're surrounded by God's favor
And supplied for by His hand.

It is not a place of works,
That in it any man should boast.
It's a place of faith and power
Sanctioned by the Holy Ghost.

It is a place of blessing,
Where we prosper and succeed,
Activating grace through faith,
To meet our every need.

In this place is help divine
For every situation,
To reach the one who lives next door
Or to affect another nation.

The attributes of God are here,
Poured out like living water.
Freely you may flow in them,
Oh, faithful son and daughter.

It's a place where we're forbearing,
Ministering grace to all who'll hear.
It's a place of love and power,
Never a place of fear.

Here His beautiful appearance
Becomes reflected in our face.
We are filled with His compassion,
When we're standing in His grace.

It's here that we are thankful,
Truly grateful from our hearts,
Living in His covenant kindness,
Where strength and wisdom He imparts.

His grace ... it is sufficient
To cleanse us from all sin,
If we will just receive Him
And choose to enter in.

Here we walk in victory
Quickened by the Spirit,
Empowered now to live the Word,
Not to simply hear it.

Father, I pray for Your gifts to be released upon
each person reading this who has a hunger and

thirst to go into new realms of creativity with You. I pray for the poetic prophetic to come alive and reach a generation with the rhythm and style that it takes for that generation to hear Your voice.

In Jesus' name,

Amen!

Chapter 11

PROPHETIC PROCLAMATION AND DECLARATION

Job 22:28-30

Thou shalt also decree a thing, and it shall be established unto thee: and the light shall shine upon thy ways. When men are cast down, then thou shalt say, There is lifting up; and he shall save the humble person. He shall deliver the island of the innocent: and it is delivered by the pureness of thine hands.

The Bible tells us that when we decree a thing, the Lord will establish it for us. Therefore we need to make bold declarations over our generation, our children, our homes, our families, our finances, our ministries and our jobs. When we declare something according to God's heart and will, He will kiss it and anoint it. In this chapter, I will show how we can change the world around us through bold prophetic proclamations and declarations.

The tongue can be used to either bless or curse. There is power in your heart and in the prophetic word that can come forth from your lips. Learn to use your words well.

When I am driving in my car, I encourage myself in the Lord. I make declarations over myself. I say such things as:

"I am filled with the Holy Spirit and, therefore, am empowered to do the will and the work of the Lord."
"I am healthy, wealthy and wise."

This is the hour for us to decree and declare and stake our claim to the fullness of our inheritance. Let's remember that God is the Great Encourager and not the great discourager. When faced with great battles and opposition, David encouraged himself in the Lord. For instance, when his own men turned against him, the Bible says that he knew what to do. We, too, are called to be a prophetic generation that encourages ourselves and others.

Proclamation and declaration are one of the eleven realms and channels of the prophetic that I spoke of in Chapter 4. I believe that our generation, the end-time warriors and handmaidens, will utilize this channel of prophecy to usher in the great end-time move of the Spirit of God.

As I have noted in previous chapters, I had the honor of working with and sitting under the teaching of Ruth Ward Heflin, one of the great prophetic voices to the nations, and she said that prophecy is the voice of revival. John the

Baptist said, *"Prepare ye the way of the Lord"* (Matthew 3:3), and this is the way we do it, by proclaiming and declaring His Word.

God's Word is sharper than any two-edged sword. Therefore, a prophetic declaration is a trumpet sound that pushes back the darkness and makes a way where there has seemed to be no way.

When we pray, we need to pray as though what we are believing for were. We must call it into being by declaring it. When we come into agreement with the Word of God and we then decree a thing, it shall be established.

Whether we are praying over our children, our finances or the obstacles and hindrances in our life, let us step beyond just asking; let's begin to make bold declarations. Let us declare the Word and the will of the Lord!

Sometimes I hear people praying, "Oh God, please help my little Billy. You know my Billy. He can't seem to help himself. Please help him. He is very weak. He can't seem to pick the right friends, and he can't say no to drugs and alcohol. Oh please help my Billy!" When we pray like that, we're not really blessing Billy; we are cursing him. The tongue that blesses is the same tongue that curses! Let's begin to bless our children by declaring the Word of the Lord over them.

The Lord called Gideon a *"mighty man of valor"* (Judges 6:12), declaring that over him when Gideon was hiding from his enemies and trying to find foot for his desperate family. Since you and I are speaking on behalf of the Lord, let us speak blessings and not curses. By our declarations and proclamations, we can make a way for Christ's Kingdom to come.

When we arise each morning, let us command our morning, as the Bible teaches in Job:

Job 38:12-13

Hast thou commanded the morning since thy days; and caused the dayspring to know his place; that it might take hold of the ends of the earth, that the wicked might be shaken out of it?

We can use God's Word to push the enemy back. In this way, we are commanding the morning, calling the day into being, call forth God's will for each day, calling our covenant blessings down. Do it for your own life, but also do it for your ministry and for your loved ones. Your words will be felt to the ends of the earth, and wickedness and demonic influence will be removed.

Come on, Brother! Come on, Sister! Declare it! Proclaim it! Call it into being! Now is the time!

When you speak, let the winds come from the four corners of the earth to carry your words forth. Let the power of the Spirit that dwells within you, the Spirit of Power, the Spirit of Might and the Spirit of Wisdom, be released. Speak into the air, and your words will change the spiritual climate in the earth.

Didn't God declare that we should have dominion over all things? He has called us to rule and reign. We are meant to be seated in heavenly places with Christ Jesus, and He has put everything under our feet.

There is power in your tongue. There is power in your prayer. There is power in the prophetic. It is one of the greatest ways to demonstrate the power that God has given us. He said that He has given us all power and all authority. So, let's use it. Let's declare His will!

I declare right now the year of harvest over you and yours. This is your year of restoration. This is your year of family salvation. God hasn't just saved you. I declare His Word over you, and that Word is for your entire family.

I declare that this is the year of the favor of the Lord for your life. In the midst of everything, you are called to be the head and not the tail, the lender and not the borrower. You are called for such a time as this. You are a child of the harvest!

I declare the harvest that I see in you. You will begin to receive divine appointments and destiny encounters. Nothing in your life will ever again be by chance because *"the steps of a good man are ordered by the Lord"* (Psalm 37:23). I declare the blessing of the Lord over you, that everything you put your hand to will prosper.

And I challenge you to begin declaring God's Word today. Stop your stinking thinking. Stop begging God in prayer. You are the King's kid. You are covered by the blood of the Lamb. You can go boldly to the Throne of Grace, and whatever you ask in Jesus' name that is according to His will *shall* be given unto you.

Father, I pray that Your people would know the great inheritance that You have for them. I pray for them to have an increase of Your wisdom and that the eyes of their understanding would be opened.
In Jesus' mighty name,
Amen!

Chapter 12

RELATIONSHIPS: THE PROPHET, THE PEOPLE AND THE LORD

Hebrews 13:17

Obey them that have the rule over you, and submit yourselves.

In this chapter, I want to summarize what I feel is necessary for the prophetic voice to operate within the Church.

First, our primary relationship is with the Lord. We need to be disciplined in our prayer life and disciplined in the Word, for we are meant for an intimate relationship with Him. All else flows from that relationship.

The prophetic voice is a serious position in the Church, not to be taken lightly, either by the one giving the prophetic word or the one receiving the prophetic word. As I obey God in bringing forth the word the Spirit gives me, I will be tested in that word. Therefore, we must be willing to submit to our leaders and know that our word will be judged and *should* be judged.

For those receiving a word, God is looking into your future. The word may not be for today or tomorrow. It could be for weeks, months or even years down the road. However, it is my responsibility to bring forth what the Lord is speaking to me.

I must emphasize this: as a prophetic voice, I must be sensitivity to the rest of the Body, so that I can relate properly to the people I minister to. And my gift must always be ministered in love.

For too many years, prophetic people have used their gifting, calling and anointing as an excuse for not walking in right relationships with others. Even, at times, it has been used as an excuse for rude behavior and an aloof attitude. It is time we realize that developing and maintaining right and healthy relationships is key to successful ministry of any type. This is even more important when ministering in the areas of the prophetic and the supernatural. It is our willingness to step into relationship with other members of the Body that will actually allow us to be received and make an impact on others.

But, let us deal with first things first: It is important that we know that we are not called as a spokesperson to the Church. Instead, we are called as a spokesperson *for the Lord* to the Church. Therefore, our primary relationship needs to be cultivating that intimate walk with the One who leads us, guides us and directs us. Cultivating this relationship on a daily basis is crucial. We need to develop this relationship through prayer, through fellowship and through the vulnerability of walking in humility before the Lord.

There is no substitute for a disciplined prayer life, and there is no substitute for being solid in God's Word. Then, we must seek to be unencumbered by the weighty personal and human circumstances that surround us.

In addition to my relationship with the Lord, I must also develop and maintain a right relationship with others in the Body of Christ, particularly with those who are in leadership or in an authority position within the Body. Why? Because one of the most common and unfortunately of the common criticisms of those who are in prophetic ministry is that they see themselves as Lone Rangers. That should never be. We were not meant to be an island. God's desire for every Christian believer is that we be interconnected and interrelated properly in the Body with right accountability and balance in our lives.

For prophetic people, one of the most important of relationships on the local church level is staying in right relationship with the pastor. This takes a lot of grace, wisdom and patience, since many times we are viewing things from different perspectives. Even though we may have the same motive and the same objective, we often come at it from different directions. We need to prefer one another and try to understand one another and the God-given responsibilities that each of us has been assigned.

We must learn to communicate with each other, pray together and pray for one another, because the pastor-prophet relationship can often make or break a ministry.

Again, the Word of God clearly tells us:

Hebrews 13:17

Obey them that have the rule over you and submit yourselves.

As a prophetic voice, I must realize that anytime I speak publicly on behalf of the Lord, my words and my life will be tried and tested by others, by the enemy and by the Lord. I must realize that misunderstandings will come about at times because of the things I say, the methods I use or the attitude I have as I minister. It's my responsibility to bring forth the Word of the Lord in such a way that those who hear it will clearly understand what the Lord is saying to us, and (according to 1 Corinthians 14:29) realize that those in authority are called upon to judge that word. If you are not willing to submit to this judgment, then you will have a very difficult time answering the call and should probably not even take the first steps. Those who are in authority are required and responsible to do their part as well.

To be prophetic, it would seem a great benefit to be sensitive spiritually and emotionally, especially to the prompting of the Lord. But we also need to make sure that we are not thin-skinned. Being thin-skinned can allow a spirit of offense to come upon us and hinder us, not just in our gifting and calling, but also in our basic Christian life and walk.

John Bevere deals with this issue of the spirit of offense in his wonderful book *The Bait of Satan.* [1] Many misunderstandings between members of the Body of Christ can result in feelings of rejection and, at times, cause us to shrink back or even question who we are in the Lord. This makes it difficult to walk in the confident relationship that is necessary to represent Christ and boldly speak on His behalf publicly. There are a few things that we can do to minimize such misunderstandings.

First, we must develop the necessary personal relationship, so that the pastor and prophet know each other's hearts.

Second, we must purpose to always submit each misunderstanding to conflict resolution, not allowing our differences to fester or linger in our hearts. Instead, we must sit down together and legitimately communicate with each other our needs, thoughts and feelings. Relationships like this require time, effort and patience.

Finally, the principle requirement is sincere humility. This is not just a requirement for ministry; it is the way of Christ. If we want to operate in His grace gifts, we need His grace and favor in our daily lives. The Scriptures tell

1. Lake Mary, FL, Charisma House: 1994

us that He gives grace to the humble, but He resists the proud (see James 4:6). The Word also tells us to draw near to God, and He will draw near to us (see James 4:8). You and I both know that the Word works.

Far too many pastors seem to require one hundred percent accuracy of any prophet, and the penalty for any failure is death. That being the case, how are prophetic voices to be raised up and trained? As prophets, we are nothing more than redeemed human beings, with all of our natural shortcomings. This needs to be understood by all.

Too often, we call someone a false prophet because we have been expecting infallibility. That's not realistic. I do believe there are false prophets and false prophecies, and we need to test the spirits and bring correction where it is needed. However, we also need to understand that the meaning of *false* is "not true, incorrect, wrong, untruthful, lying, misleading or not real." Often a person who gives a wrong prophetic word might better be described as "inaccurate or not exact," which has far different implications.

We can all make mistakes, so a great part of the judging we do as pastors must be of an individual's motives. Nothing that is done with wrong motives will prosper, but people with good motives do makes mistakes.

There are words that are spoken prophetically in the realm of declaration and proclamation that are not properly conceived or perceived, and there are also words of presumptuousness. By that I mean something is taken for granted that may actually come from one's own soul rather than from the Spirit realm. It may be a product of the mind, will and emotions, a personal opinion or conviction.

But be careful. Pastors who oversee prophetic activity and those who receive a prophetic word must realize that when a prophetic word is spoken, it often seems quite impossible, and we cannot imagine how it could happen. However, in the fullness of and the perfection of time, it will come to pass.

Isaiah spoke some of the most powerful Messianic prophecies ever recorded, but he went to his grave with those words yet unfulfilled. It was hundreds of years later that the word of the Lord spoke through him came to pass in the manifestation of the birth, life and death of our Lord Jesus Christ. We know that Isaiah was not a false prophet.

Finally, there have been times when we, as prophetic people, don't do all that we can to take time to be with and get to know and understand the people we minister to. Obviously, this is not always possible. But we need to do all that we can, to cultivate a Christ-like personality and relate properly to the people in the Church, not just the ones we like, but also the ones we don't. Let us commit ourselves to developing right and real relationships.

As prophetic people, we must be touchable, open and vulnerable, so that God's people will realize that as it was with Elijah, so it is with us. The Bible says, in James 5:17, that Elijah *"was a man subject to like passions as we are."* Let us remember that you and I are only special in God, so let us not think more highly of ourselves then we ought to think. Let us remember that the greatest of gifts is love and that without it we are an empty cymbal, just another voice.

It's time to mature, not just in our gift, but also in our character. Let us strive to do as Paul. He said:

1 Corinthians 13:11-13

When I was a child, I spake as a child, I understood as a child: but when I became a man, I put away childish things. For now we see through a glass, darkly; but then face to face: now I know in part; but then shall I know even as also I am known. And now abideth faith, hope, charity, these three; but the greatest of these is charity.

Father, I thank You for the prophetic voice, and I thank You, Lord for accountability. I pray, Father, for maturity in the people You are raising up in this hour, not just in our giftings, but in our character. I pray that Your people would walk in integrity as they administer Your giftings and speak forth that which they hear You saying.

In Jesus' name.
Amen!

Chapter 13

THE ROLE OF THE PROPHETIC VOICE IN THE MARKETPLACE

Revelation 1:6

And hath made us kings and priests unto God and His Father; to him be glory and dominion for ever and ever. Amen.

As I have been declaring, God is raising up a great army in these days, an army of kings and priests to reach out to others. There are many people who never enter the doors of a church, but God's voice must be heard from the church to the marketplace. In this chapter, I will show how we can reach beyond the four walls of the church with our prophetic voices.

That's what Jesus did. He went out into the marketplace. He prophesied to a woman at the well in Samaria one day, and her life was forever changed.

Philip met a eunuch one day when he was on a trip. The man was the Treasurer of Ethiopia, and when he saw

Philip reading the book of Isaiah, he was intrigued. Philip won him to the Lord and baptized him in water.

Joseph was a businessman, and Paul was a tent-maker. Each of us can represent the Lord is our sphere of influence and beyond, but in order to be effective, we must do it prophetically.

The prophetic disarms those who might normally never be open to the Gospel in a traditional sense. This is the time for the prophetic voice to go forth and give hope and life to a world that badly needs the Lord. We are to be a light on a hill for all the world to see. Let us be that light in the marketplace. Let us be the voice of God infiltrating places that only you can go and reaching people that only you can reach.

Does the prophetic voice really have a role and a function in the marketplace? The answer is a resounding "yes!" As five-fold ministers in this season and as an end-time army of ministers, we must understand God's purposes, and, sooner or later, we need to do our job and prepare or perfect the saints to do the work of ministry. Part of that ministry is in the marketplace. Those who are trying to have an impact in our society need to hear the voice of the Lord, the direction of the Lord, and the strategy of the Lord.

In John 17, the Bible clearly tells us that we are sent to the world in the same way the Father sent Jesus into the world. We are not to be *of* the world, but we are certainly *in* this world for a divine reason. We need to be a light and a voice in the marketplace.

The question is not, "Am I supposed to be there?" The question is, "What is my role there? How do I exercise my authority there? How do I let my light shine there?" The following points should help to define and understand this role and maximize the impact you can make on your world.

First and foremost, my character and integrity will have a direct effect on the way I am received in the marketplace. How I conduct myself in my affairs before others is paramount. I have to understand that people in the marketplace have a different sense of values and are looking at life and playing by a different set of rules. I have to base my life on the biblical principles I stand for, even if I appear, at times, quite different than what people are accustomed to.

Even though I have different foundational principles, the Lord knows (and I need to know) what appeals to others, what will get their attention. If the Lord is actually teaching us to be fishers of men, He doesn't just want us to drop a hook in the water and wait to see what happens. We must use different bait to attract different fish. For this, I need wisdom, strategy and revelation from the Lord, but the foundation is that my character must be unyielding and right before others.

The second key is to look for opportunities. I cannot expect to have an impact on society sitting in my living room or always surrounding myself with church people. I have to get out into the marketplace, so I must begin to develop relationships with Christians who are working in that environment and will give me the opportunity to partner with them in the harvest field they're in. I need to begin to cultivate relationships with people in my congregation who can afford me those relationships.

Let me give you an example: On several occasions, a businessman, a Jewish believer who attends our church in southern Ontario, arranged for me to meet some of his customers. They knew that he was a believer by his life and witness, and I have a great relationship with him. He arranged a time for me to meet with these particular customers, who happened to own a supermarket, and to prophesy over their family and their business.

The Lord spoke to me about their roots and humble beginnings and also of His present-day vision for them. It was an impactful and very spiritual moment. We spent an hour with them and their leadership staff. This actually enhanced my friend's witness and business relationship with these people, for they enjoyed the presence of the Lord.

My friend has done this on many other occasions as well. It helps him to evangelize and have an impact on the lives of the people he meets. The relationships I am looking to nurture and develop are centers of influence, for this can open doors of opportunity for me to minister to others in their realm of authority.

Another example: I ministered to the hairdresser of one of my congregants. She brought me to her home, and I ministered to her whole family.

Another influential person in my life brought me to a friend who was a college administrator. He was not a Christian, but I was able to minister to him. This opened a great door, not just in his life, but it also opened up connections that impacted our ministry as well.

As a prophetic voice, I have to make myself available and take advantage of as many of these opportunities as possible. I have to let my voice be heard wherever it can be heard.

Third, as a prophet, I need to bring a sure word about future economic conditions, so that people who are under my spiritual influence and are looking to expand their business, invest in a new home, start a new business venture or are contemplating making any other investment, will be able to have a reliable view of both the present and future economic trends. Unfortunately, many times I have heard what amounted to fearful predictions, and these have caused members of the Body of Christ to miss golden opportunities to prosper, all because a prophet didn't understand the timing to release the revelation of the Lord.

We begin each year with a Watch Night prophetic service, where we prophesy the words the Lord gives us for the New Year. I almost always include what the Lord is speaking about the coming economic climate.

Fourth, I need to provide training and equipping for marketplace ministers, so that they fully understand their role. These are important principles that the Lord has been giving us for some time now. Now is the time to equip the marketplace ministers and train them and support them properly, to fulfill their destiny.

Last, I try to speak prophetically into the lives of those who get outside of the realm of the nuclear church and into the marketplace, whether it's in education, government, entertainment, the medical field, etc. I want to speak words of encouragement, comfort and exhortation regularly into their lives.

More than anything else that comes from the pulpit the Lord has given me, I want to constantly affirm people and their importance in God's agenda, so that they will know they are received and accepted by Him (and by us) in their role. I understand the importance of this personal affirmation because, for more than twenty years, I was a marketplace minister and did not feel understood or appreciated in my call—other than the fact that I was expected to sow financially into the church.

That is certainly part of the role of a Christian in the marketplace, but it is not the totality of his role. I must continue to bring the role of marketplace ministry to the attention of all believer, enhancing their standing and confirming their place in both the church and the marketplace.

If you are a prophetic voice in this season, or if you are in the leadership role of the office gift of the prophet, I want to encourage you to use that voice and that gift for the edification of your brothers and sisters who are in marketplace ministry. If you are a marketplace minister, hear the voice of the Lord. Don't just hear it; heed it. Bring your life and your business into alignment with His words and begin to cooperate with the Lord to bring all that He has spoken to fulfillment.

This is our hour of impact, the purpose of revival is transformation, and he gift of prophecy is the voice of re-vival. Let us begin to use it to clearly define God's purposes and strategies to have a substantial impact beyond the four walls of the church (meaning beyond the four walls of the church building(. It's time to extend and advance the Kingdom of God into every area and focus in our society. It's time for the kings and priests to walk together and to respect the gift and call of God on each other's lives, so that we can truly partner and walk in unity and harmony in the reaping the great end-time harvest.

Father, I thank You that Your presence goes with me into the marketplace. Lord, You laid hands on the sick and healed people and prophesied in the marketplace. Father, give me boldness to bring a word of life to those who are waiting to hear words of hope. Lord, we are the Church, and the world is our mission field. Help us to encourage and edify those who are in the marketplace for Your name's sake.

In Jesus' name we pray,
Amen!

Chapter 14

PROPHETIC INTERCESSION

Matthew 21:13

It is written, My house shall be called the house of prayer.

The words *prophetic* and *intercessor* are synonymous, for intercession is one of the main functions of the prophet. We are vessels releasing God's will on Earth. We are on the frontlines, pioneering in the Spirit.

Prophetic intercession is to know the heartbeat of God, entering into His presence and hearing His voice on what His will is in a given situation in people's lives. It is our job to hear and see and then go into warfare, if need be, and pray God's will over that situation.

God is raising up a new breed of intercessors, prophetic intercessors willing to go to places in prayer and intercession, willing to stay up and pray all night, willing to fast, willing to do whatever it takes to bring about God's will. Our call is not just to focus on ourselves, but rather, to focus on God's heart. In this chapter, I want to show you just how important this ministry is in these end times.

My primary calling as a prophetic voice is that of an intercessor. Therefore, personal prayer and intimacy with God have always been an important part of my Christian walk.

When I am selecting a leader, I look for what I believe God wants in a leader. I first look for a basic foundation for the Christian life. Then, of course, I look for character, the fruit of the Spirit, along with skills, gifts and talents related to the leader's role and responsibility.

The basic foundation of a Christian walk is to be a man or woman who has a working knowledge of the Word of God, along with daily discipline to continue to seek the Lord in His Word. Secondly, I want to see that the person has a real prayer life. And, finally, I want to know that they are connected in a local body of believers.

Now, when I said "a real prayer life," let me explain a little what I mean. Prayer is not all about discipline and ritual; it's about relationship, communication and intimacy. I like what Paul said about his prayer life, that he prayed *"without ceasing"* (Romans 1:9, 1 Thessalonians 2:13 and 5:17 and 2 Timothy 1:3). He was *"instant in prayer"* (Romans 12:12). The Lord wants us to be *"instant in season"* and *"out of season"* (2 Timothy 4:2). It's not about how long I pray, but rather that I maintain a fresh relationship with the Lord, a relationship with ample communication, and that I realize that He never leaves me or forsakes me. This doesn't mean we don't have need seasons of fasting and prayer, but let's focus, first and foremost, on the attitude of prayer.

In order for my prayer life to be relational and real, it must be a two-way communication. I don't want to end up with me always doing all the talking, but rather that I keep a right attitude while praying. What is a right attitude? It is not just praying my desires, but also praying what is on the Lord's heart, His agenda, His timetable.

God has promised that if I delight myself in Him, He will give me the very desires of my heart. I believe that promise. But the first part of that verse, the qualifier (if I delight myself in Him), is just as important as the promise. He will do His part as we do ours.

I'm sure that most readers want to know how deep they are in their Christian walk and relationship with the Lord. To me, one of the primary indicators of depth is my prayer life, how much time I spend with the Lord, and what is my attitude in prayer. In other words, what am I praying about and believing for? Is it all about me and mine? Is it about the shallow things of my heart's desire? Or am I seeking God's heart and His desire? Am I seeking for His will to be done and His Kingdom to come?

There are many types of prayer. For instance, there is the prayer for the sick of James 5:13-16. There is prayer for our enemy, as the Lord directed us in Matthew 5. Also, there is praying in the Spirit according to 1 Corinthians14:14. There's the prayer of agreement of Deuteronomy 32:30 that multiplies power and effectiveness. There is also prayer for the nations, praying for our leaders, and according to the Lord's specific request, prayer for Jerusalem. There is your personal prayer of petition for your needs or the needs of your loved ones. There is also a deeper level of prayer, and that is the prayer of intercession.

Regardless of the style or type of prayer, Jesus said in Matthew 21:13, *"It is written, My house shall be called the house of prayer."* To my way of thinking, the call and ministry of the intercessor is as important to the operation, leadership and success of the Church as the five-fold offices, which are the full expression of the ministry life of Christ as He walked the earth.

Intercession is actually the ministry of Christ today. He is the Head of all intercession, for He is the Great Intercessor. The Bible shows us that Christ is seated at the right hand of the Father making intercession for us right now (see Romans 8:34).

In this season, I believe, God is again looking for men and woman who fit the description of Ezekiel 22:30:

Ezekiel 22:30

And I sought for a man among them, that should make up the hedge, and stand in the gap before me for the land, that I should not destroy it: but I found none.

Can the Lord find such a person in you and in me? In this hour, He is calling His intercessors to the forefront, to stand their watch upon the wall, to prophetically engage the enemy—both afar off and at the gate and walls of the community of God. Will you answer this call?

When I go before the Lord in prophetic intercession, I first enter with praise and worship. This is the way we enter into God's presence and then into His glory. That is the place where revelation is, and where He begins to show us His heart. Then, when I have sensed God's heart and desire, I start praying it back to Him.

Do you want to hit some home-runs in prayer? Then pray the will of God. When you go to prayer, pray with a Kingdom vision. Begin to look at your prayer life and the requests you make to God from the viewpoint of the King.

This is an hour for intercessors to go to war. As we have seen, we are called to be the great end-time warriors who are quick to go to battle and quick to go to the throne. Prayer is one of the greatest spiritual weapons we have at our disposal, prayer that is birthed in God's glory and presence. Warring with worship is the highest form of warfare. And a man who *doesn't* pray is no better off than a man who *can't* pray.

There are some great books on prayer and intercession. A few that have inspired me and helped me to gain an understanding of the purposes and methods of prayer are: *Intercession* by Joy Dawson, [2] *Intercession* by Watchman Nee, [3] and *Cross Pollination* by Lila Terhune. [4] Lila was over intercession at Brownsville Assembly of God and was the first person to teach me about this all-important subject. I became a part of her intercessory prayer team and served

2. Seattle, WA, YWAM Publishing: 1997
3. With Witness Lee, Living Stream Ministry: 1991
4. Shippensburg, PA, Destiny Image Publishers: 1998

for two years in the midst of the famous revival there. Lila is a wonderful woman of prayer, a great warrior and has a great prophetic gift.

Whether you're in the office of the prophet or operating in your prophetic gift, one of the important realms and channels of prophecy is prophetic intercession. The Word of God is clear:

Jeremiah 27:18-19

> *But if they be prophets, and if the word of the LORD be with them, let them now make intercession to the LORD of hosts, that the vessels which are left in the house of the LORD, and in the house of the king of Judah, and at Jerusalem, go not to Babylon. For thus saith the LORD of hosts concerning the pillars, and concerning the sea, and concerning the bases, and concerning the residue of the vessels that remain in this city.*

When does God tell us to make intercession? NOW! We are to pray for those who are in the House of the Lord (our brothers and sisters), and also for the House of Judah (the worshipers, worship leaders and worship team), and for Jerusalem (representing the council and leaders) so that they will not go back to Babylon, a place of captivity, a place of confusion. We are to pray that they do not backslide.

God says to pray for *"the pillars"* (the deacons and the elders). Then He says to pray for *"the sea,"* which is the multitude of people and *"the bases,"* which are the extended church, the outreach ministers, the marketplace ministers, those who work in counseling centers and those who house the homeless and feed the hungry. Finally, it tells us to pray for our cities and all who live there.

I want to encourage you, exhort you and challenge you to a higher place in your prayer life in the Lord. It is a deeper place, the place in His heart, the place of prophetic intercession.

May the Lord richly bless you. May He anoint you afresh today. May He light your heart ablaze with a hunger to seek Him. I pray that, by the power of His Spirit, He will draw you to a deeper place in Him, that He will light up your prayer closet like the 4th of July.

Father, I pray that You will impart a greater desire for Your people to enter into Your presence with praise and worship and then enter into the secret place, where they can hear Your voice and know Your heart, a place where they can learn to pray Your will and become world-changers through prophetic intercession.

In Jesus' name,
Amen!

Chapter 15

LEARNING TO OPERATE IN THE VISIONARY REALM

Proverbs 29:18

Where there is no vision, the people perish, but he that keepeth the law, happy is he.

Part of becoming a prophetic voice is gaining access to the visionary realm. Most prophets of old saw before they spoke. Then they spoke what they were seeing.

And God not only spoke in visions to the people of the Old Testament; He continued to speak to His people in visions in the New Testament; and He continues to speak today to many in this way. He is truly *"the same yesterday, today and forever."*

As a prophet, moving in the visionary realm allows me to see things before they can be seen with the natural eye. It allows me to see much further than I can see in the natural. Seeing in the visionary realm gives me dreams and hopes for the future and also strategies to achieve the will, heart and purpose of God.

Joshua and Caleb ran with a vision. They did not see themselves as grasshoppers in their own sight, as the other Israelite spies did (see Numbers 13:33). Their visionary ability told them that those giants could easily be defeated. These men were God's visionaries. They knew and understood God's promises and were willing to run with the prophetic vision they had caught. They trusted God when, in the natural, what God was showing them might not have made sense. Their focus was not on the giants, but on God.

The visionary realm is a prophetic realm of the Spirit and one of the ways the Lord uses to speak to man. Our text verse reveals an important spiritual truth or spiritual law. Spiritual laws govern the spiritual realm just as natural or scientific laws (such as Gravity, Inertia and Relativity) govern the natural realm. Our ignorance or indifference to a natural or spiritual law doesn't change the fact that there is a cause and effect related to our activity in that realm.

I am a simple person. When I first heard this scripture spoken in church, I was disappointed. I didn't have a vision, so I didn't understand what vision was. This led me to conclude that I was doomed to perish.

The Proverbs are spiritual laws that can affect our lives in a practical way, and the Bible is a guide to successful Christian living. The book of Proverbs gives us a practical view of how to apply these principles to our lives. It is absolutely essential that we have an understanding of vision and the visionary realm.

We need to know how to catch a vision, how to cast the vision and how to run with the vision. We need to know the difference between a personal vision, a corporate vision and a Kingdom vision. We need to be able to spiritually discern between the vision of God and the vision of man.

One of the fastest ways to find yourself lost is by following someone who is going to a different destination. In that way, it is easy to be distracted or even deceived. When God's vision is revealed, His sheep hear His voice. Those with a like spirit and like heart receive a witness in their spirit that confirms His Word.

When the corporate, or Kingdom, vision of God is revealed or cast, those of like heart will find their piece and part of the vision, God's will for their personal lives. The vision that God has for each of us will then show the way the parts of the Body of Christ are to fit together for the fulfillment of the entire vision.

THE VISION OF GOD AND THE VISIONARY REALM

The vision of God reveals the heart or the purpose of God while the vision of man reveals the heart or purpose of man in a particular situation. When people gather around the vision of God, they gather around the heart and purpose of God for that particular person or persons, area, season or city, etc. In the visionary realm, when we gather around the vision of man, we are clearly not gathering around God; we are gathering around man; and the result will neither glorify God nor benefit us.

Man's vision is measured in time, but God's vision is measured in eternity. His purposes are not carnal in nature, but spiritual. A prophetic people, a prophetic generation, will not only hear the voice of God, but will also respond to Him, capturing the vision and carrying it out. They will run with the vision.

Since God is not only the Author of our faith, but also the Finisher of our faith and Jehovah Jireh our Provider, He will bring together all the parts, pieces, people and resources necessary, not just to birth His vision, but also to build, sustain and maintain His vision.

What has happened to Eagle Worldwide Ministries in recent years has very little to do with any man or woman. In fact, most of what God has done through our fellowship of churches has been accomplished when I was nowhere around. The visionary was nowhere to be found, but that didn't matter. It was not the vision of man, but of God.

EXAMPLES OF WORKS BIRTHED IN THE VISIONARY REALM

The birthing of our churches, the birthing of our Retreat and Revival Centre, our Summer Camp, our Intern Program, our King's Way Blessing Centre, our outreach ministries—Centre for Excellence, Gage Park Outreaches, the missionary travel team and the Network of Ministries have all been the result of a vision from God. All of these aspects of the ministry were birthed strictly through revelation given to us by the Lord through dreams, visions and the prophetic word.

Not only was the revelation given to us; it was also confirmed by revelation from multiple sources, people, who, at the time, had no idea what the Lord was speaking to us.

The Lord will always confirm His word. He sends men and women of like heart and like spirit, men and women who have captured the vision and fulfilled a portion of their personal vision and mission in life and are now concentrating on the corporate and Kingdom vision of God. This is all part of God's plan for multiplication and duplication.

THE PLAN FOR THE HARVEST

Most men dream big dreams, but few actually wake up and make their dreams become reality. Fulfillment usually comes with those who have the understanding and the relationship with God to of apply the vision, with the resources He sends, to develop a mission, a strategy and an action plan.

It is by active faith that we give our vision wings. It is by the unity of the Spirit and cooperating together in that Spirit of unity that the commanded blessing of God is brought forth, as David declared in Psalm 133:

Psalm 133:1-3

Behold, how good and how pleasant it is for brethren to dwell together in unity! It is like the precious ointment upon the head, that ran down upon the beard, even Aaron's beard: that went down to the skirts of his garments; As the dew of Hermon, and as the dew that descended upon the mountains of Zion: for there the LORD commanded the blessing, even life for evermore.

We achieve this unity by learning how to pray together, how to plan together and how to work together to fulfill God's vision. This is His will for us and is reflected in Jesus' prayer recorded by John:

John 17:20-23

Neither pray I for these alone, but for them also which shall believe on me through their word; that they all may be one; as thou, Father, art in me, and I in thee, that they also may be one in us: that the world may believe that thou hast sent me.

And the glory which thou gavest me I have given them; that they may be one, even as we are one: I in them, and thou in me, that they may be made perfect in one; and that the world may know that thou hast sent me, and hast loved them, as thou hast loved me.

When we become distracted, discouraged, divided or in some measure of disunity because of our personal initiative, ambition or pride, we are not necessarily under a curse because Christ took the curse of the Law upon Himself (see Galatians 3:13). Still, the blessing of God and the anointing of God are obviously not there. What we must do is recapture the vision and blessing of God. When we find ourselves discouraged, distracted or off course, let's capture again the vision of God, not the vision of man. Let's unite again around His vision.

There are a lot of good things that we can do, but we need to do the "God Thing." Capture His vision, understand His mission. Then develop a strategy and write out a plan of action to accomplish it. That's what Habakkuk did:

Habakkuk 2:1-5

I will stand upon my watch, and set me upon the tower, and will watch to see what he will say unto me, and what I shall answer when I am reproved.

And the LORD answered me, and said, Write the vision, and make it plain upon tables, that he may run that readeth it. For the vision is yet for an appointed time, but at the end it shall speak, and not lie: though it tarry, wait for it; because it will surely come, it will not tarry.

Behold, his soul which is lifted up is not upright in him: but the just shall live by his faith.

Yea also, because he transgresseth by wine, he is a proud man, neither keepeth at home, who enlargeth his desire as hell, and is as death, and cannot be satisfied, but gathereth unto him all nations, and heapeth unto him all people.

We must all run with the Lord's vision in a spirit of unity and harmony. Following God is not complicated. It is not necessarily easy, but it is also not complicated. It is thoughts from the heart and mind of man that complicate the simplicity of the heart and purpose of God. He is not hard to catch, nor is His vision. He is not running away from us. He wants us to find Him. But, let's chase after God, not after man. Let's capture the vision of God, and then let's run with it.

Lord, I thank You for the visionary realm, and I pray that each reader would walk in the fullness of all that You have for them. I pray for our eyes to be opened to Your vision, measured in eternity. I pray that as our eyes see with Your eyes, Your perspective, we will run with the vision for our lives and accomplish much for You in this world.

Father, I pray that we would become those who know that with You nothing is impossible, and that as we keep our eyes on You, we can do all things through Christ who strengthens us.

In Jesus' name,
Amen!

Chapter 16

UNDERSTANDING END-TIME PROPHECY

John 1:14

And the Word was made flesh, and dwelt among us, (and we beheld his glory, the glory as of the only begotten of the Father,) full of grace and truth.

Revelation 19:10

For the testimony of Jesus is the spirit of prophecy.

One thing is for sure: the Bible tells us that no man knows the day or hour of the return of Christ. The Word of God is our final authority, and all earthly authority must line up with His Word.

One day in 2011, I turned on the television, and there was a report on the news that the end of the world was coming on May 21. Unfortunately, billboards had been erected to that effect and people were going door to door warning anyone who would listen that the Rapture was about to take place and then the Judgment Day would come. As a result of these warnings, some people had already left their jobs. How sad this was to me! We are in the end times, but this is not the end of time. In this chapter, I want to focus your attention on the important elements of end-time prophecy.

The Word of God tells us in Matthew 24:36:

But of that day and hour, no one knows, not even the angels of heaven, but my Father only.

Verse 44 says:

Therefore be ye also ready: for in such an hour as ye think not the Son of man cometh.

One of the eleven realms or channels of the prophetic that I teach about is end-time prophecy (see Chapter 5). Peter declared:

2 Peter 1:21
For the prophecy came not in old time by the will of man: but holy men of God spake as they were moved by the Holy Ghost.

The prophecy of the Scriptures is not for private and personal interpretation. It is recorded so that God's people will be able to discern the times and seasons in His heart, and so that we can prepare our hearts for the great and dreadful Day of the Lord.

The Bible clearly tells us that in the last days, if it were possible, even the very elect would be deceived (see Matthew 245:24). Therefore, we who are seeking hard after the heart of God need to be especially discerning, as we move deeper and higher in revelation knowledge. We must stand fully rooted in the Word of God, and we must test every spirit.

In recent years, I have been exposed to many books written concerning end-time revelation. In some cases, I have been very disappointed to find that what was in those books was not much more than prophetic nonsense. It is so important that we test each revelation with the Word of God, for this is the only real source of Truth. The Bible is a "more sure" Word!

I firmly believe that what we need to concern ourselves with in this season is realizing, by the signs of the times, that we are standing on the threshold of the greatest harvest ever known to man and also on the threshold of the great end-time battle, prophetically proclaimed, between good and evil. We need to allow the Lord to prepare our hearts and position us, so that we will be personally ready, and then we need to concentrate on raising up laborers for the harvest.

Jesus Himself, in Mathew 24, when asked privately by His disciples, spoke very forthrightly about the signs of the Second Coming and the end of the age. He told them to take heed that no man deceive them (see verse 4). That entire chapter is important for us, as end-time warriors and handmaidens, to read and digest. In this way, we can see and understand for ourselves the season in the heart of the Lord.

The wars and rumors of wars, the pestilences, famines and earthquakes, false prophets rising up and the hearts of many waxing cold ... these are all important signs. We can turn on CNN or Fox News or pick up a local newspaper and hear the latest reports of the conflict and turmoil in the Middle East and know in our hearts that we are quickly moving closer to that great and dreadful day. Not only are there natural disasters; but look at what man has done to the ecology and economy by his ignorance, neglect, greed and general moral decay.

The terrible release of oil into the Gulf of Mexico in 2010 has had devastating effects, some that may not be known for many years. This is an hour when the hearts of men and nations are being weighed in the balance and found wanting. We are at a moment in which all are being tried and tested, a time when you and I need to be steadfast in the Lord, knowledgeable in His Word and diligent in our quest of His will for our lives.

End-time prophecy is one of my personal pursuits. I enjoy studying these mysteries. But, in this season in my teaching and preaching, the Lord has me focused on preparing the saints as laborers for the end-time harvest.

We can certainly see the present-day Church in each of the seven churches that Jesus spoke to in Revelation 2 and

3. He is obviously calling us to *"come up hither"* because He wants to show us the things that are to come. The trumpet is sounding, for this is the hour that every prophet spoke about. This is the moment of the golden harvest, a time to thrust in a sharp sickle and reap.

In Revelation 14:14-20, our focus, rather than on the seals and the trumpets, the horses and the beasts, needs to be on opening our own hearts and allowing the Spirit of God to prepare us in this season for the great harvest of souls that is at hand. We must be ensuring that we will be counted worthy in that great moment, to ride with Him, the Lord of the Harvest, the King of Kings and the Lord of Lords.

Revelation 17:14 declares:

They that are with him are called, and chosen, and faithful.

Jesus said, *"Many are called but few are chosen"* (Matthew 22:14). Those who are *"chosen"* are those who choose to turn aside from the sights and sounds of this world and answer God's call, saying, "Yes, Lord, I will follow You!" The *"faithful"* are those who faithfully serve Him and persevere to the end and who, when they have done all they can do, stand believing. May you and I be counted among them—the called, the chosen and the faithful who will ride with Him!

Father, I pray that You would give us wisdom and discernment in these last days, that our eyes would be opened to Your Word and to the signs and the seasons we are in, that we would put our hands to the plow, as if You were not coming back for another thousand years, but be ready and working as if You were coming back any moment now.

Father, I pray that You would give Your people endurance, perseverance and strength, as we continue to do Your will, making disciples and taking territory for You, thus advancing Your Kingdom.

For Jesus' sake,

Amen!

Chapter 17

PRACTICING AND TEACHING PROPHETIC WORSHIP

1 Chronicles 25:1

Moreover David and the captains of the host separated to the service of the sons of Asaph, and of Heman, and of Jeduthun, who should prophesy with harps, with psalteries, and with cymbals.

1 Chronicles 25:3

Of Jeduthun, the sons of Jeduthun: Gedaliah, Zeri, Jeshaiah, Shimei, Hasabiah, and Mattithiah, six under the direction of their father Jeduthun who prophesied with a harp to give thanks and to praise the LORD.

God is looking for those who will worship Him in Spirit and in truth, those who are hungry to have an intimate relationship with Him. We are atmosphere-changers, and this is a season of high praise and of deep crying out to deep. It is our Father's passion for the Holy Spirit to take us, as individuals, into the heart of the Father and lead the entire Body of Christ into His presence. In this chapter, I want to show you how many things are accomplished in prophetic worship.

Yes, many things are accomplished through prophetic worship, as we abandon ourselves to being led by the Holy Spirit. Not only can we begin to do spiritual warfare and enter into God's glory, but we can also experience a release of the Kingdom of God on Earth and the revealing of Jesus. Prophetic worship, therefore, is something we need more teaching on.

Prophetically speaking, this is the season when God is restoring Tabernacle- and Temple-worship back to the Body of Christ, back to the Church, back to us, as individual believers. The Bible shows us in Acts 15:

Acts 15:15-17

And to this agree the words of the prophets; as it is written, After this I will return, and will build again the tabernacle of David, which is fallen down; and I will build again the ruins thereof, and I will set it up: that the residue of men might seek after the Lord, and all the Gentiles, upon whom my name is called, saith the Lord, who doeth all these things.

This describes the season we are in right now. God is rebuilding the Tabernacle of David, His House of worship.

David was a man after the Lord's own heart, both a warrior and a worshiper. He was quick to go to battle and quick to go to the throne of God for help. He built a tabernacle for God in Jerusalem, and many of the psalms we have recorded in the Bible came forth in that place.

I believe that the Tabernacle of David was the Lord's favorite House. I'm sure that He liked the wilderness Tabernacle because it was built to His exact and perfect specifications. And His presence was there. He was present also in Solomon's Temple. Can you imagine that Temple in all of its splendor? When it was finished, God so filled it with His glory that the priests couldn't even stand upright on their feet.

Still, I believe that the Tabernacle of David was God's favorite House. It had no permanent walls, and there were no veils, nothing between Him and His people, no barriers, just God and His glory to be encountered and enjoyed.

When David's Tabernacle was complete, he went to retrieve the Ark of the Covenant and brought it back into the city of Jerusalem, carried along on the shoulders of the priests and the hearts of the worshipers. That's the way we need to bring the glory of God back into the Church today. It's all about spontaneous worship, uninhibited and carried out through reckless abandon, singing the way David sang, and dancing the way David danced. This is the hour, and God's eyes are going to and fro in all the earth, looking for worshipers who will worship Him in Spirit and in truth.

Could it be possible that the Lord needs our worship? I'm sure that He doesn't. He has no ego problem. But He ordained worship and the intimate relationship it represents. He said through David:

Psalm 8:2

Out of the mouth of babes and sucklings hast thou ordained strength because of thine enemies, that thou mightest still the enemy and the avenger.

That's right: worship, prophetic worship is the highest form of warfare. So we need it. How can we have it? There are a few ways that we can experience this prophetic worship. Paul wrote to the Colossian believers:

Colossians 3:15-16

And let the peace of God rule in your hearts, to the which also ye are called in one body; and be ye thankful. Let the word of Christ dwell in you richly in all wisdom; teaching and admonishing one another in psalms and hymns and spiritual songs, singing with grace in your hearts to the Lord.

First, from the overflow of the richness of Christ within us, spring forth psalms and hymns and spiritual songs, coming forth spontaneously from our heart.

Second, in every move of the Spirit, there has been released an anointing to highlight or write new songs with a new beat and a new sound, prophetically declaring God's heart for that particular move of the Spirit. This has been true of modern revivals, such as Toronto and Brownsville, just as it was at Azusa Street. Each move has seemed to bring forth its own sound, especially anointed for that season and for that particular generation.

To accomplish this, God raises up psalmists with a creative gift for worship. In the creative and performing arts, we see worship coming forth in every expression, from the depth of the heart of man, whether it be dance, art or music. Think of the paintings by Michelangelo in the Sistine Chapel or the prophetic art that is done during worship in many of our churches today. Whether it is in concrete form or abstract, it catches the depth and meaning of the heart of God for His people in this generation. Whether it is in the quiet stillness of our heart or in vibrant contemporary song and dance, it is the same inspiration. It represents a spiritual connection between God and man that glorifies Him, softens and prepares the heart of man to yield to His will and desire and ushers in His presence.

I had the opportunity to serve with one of the greatest worshipers of our generation—Ruth Ward Heflin. She had one of the most remarkable revelations of the glory of God and the heart of worship I have ever seen. She knew God in a very special way, and she told us exactly how to usher in His presence. She said:

Praise Him until the anointing comes to worship.
Worship until you sense the glory. (The higher the praise and the deeper the worship, the greater the glory that comes).
Then stand in the glory.

That simple formula works.

Worship is more than just a song service. It is a way of life. Psalm 100 clearly tells us:

Make a joyful noise unto the LORD, all ye lands. Serve the LORD with gladness: come before his presence with singing. Know ye that the LORD he is God: it is he that hath made us, and not we ourselves; we are his people, and the sheep of his pasture. Enter into his gates with thanksgiving, and into his courts with praise: be thankful unto him, and bless his name. For the LORD is good; his mercy is everlasting; and his truth endureth to all generations.

You and I must purpose in our hearts to let the Lord remove all of our insecurities and uncertainties, so that we may begin to worship Him as never before. We are that generation that is called to usher in the Second Coming of the Lord. We are the Church, the real Church, the remnant with a heart to worship, and we are called to become the true keepers of the flame. Let us allow liberty and freedom to be birthed in our hearts, for we can no longer consider how we look before man. Let us come before the Lord, the King of Glory, with a heart of worship and adoration.

Let us come in the Spirit, for where the Spirit of the Lord is, there is liberty. Let's you and I build an altar in our hearts today. Let's rebuild the altar of David in us.

Lord, I pray that Your people would rise up in the high praise of prophetic worship, that they would enter in to the realms of praise and worship and into Your presence and experience Your glory. Lord, I pray for Your people to rise up to worship You in music and dance, with instruments and with singing and songwriting, that You may be glorified, and that Jesus would be revealed in the hearts of men and women, Your sons and daughters.

In His name,
Amen!

Chapter 18

YOUR PROPHETIC JOURNEY TO DESTINY

Ephesians 1:17-18

That the God of our Lord Jesus Christ, the Father of glory, may give unto you the spirit of wisdom and revelation in the knowledge of him: the eyes of your understanding being enlightened; that ye may know what is the hope of his calling, and what the riches of the glory of his inheritance in the saints.

It is a time to pour into a new generation that is rising up to walk in power and authority, a generation that encompasses a range of ages, from the very young, to even the strongly mature. I believe it is time for spiritual fathers and mothers to rise up and impart the vast treasures of knowledge and experience they have gained as they have traveled in this walk with our Lord.

You cannot lead someone where you have never been, but wherever you are in your journey with Him right now and with all that you have been through, know that God has been preparing you *"for such a time as this."*

In this chapter, I want to outline for you your prophetic journey. You were formed for a purpose, for a destiny, which the Bible tells us existed before the foundations of the world, and you need to stay true to that purpose. God is revealing and releasing His people, His Church. We can lead and pour into a new generation when we know that we have traveled that road and know what works.

Let's all help raise up this next generation, a generation that has been fatherless and motherless. Let us nurture them and be there for them. Let us speak into their lives and breathe life into them with the power of our words and the role model of our faith.

As we have seen, prophetically, in this current season, we are standing at the threshold of the greatest harvest ever known to man and also the greatest battle. These are the days of the harvest. These are the days of Elijah. The fields are white and ready for the reapers.

Malachi 3 and 4 clearly speak of the season we are in. This is the time when the messenger is sent with purifying fire, to purge away that which is not of the Spirit, so that the gold and the silver will remain in our lives.

Each of us is at a different place spiritually in our journey, and sometimes we have a difficult time identifying our destiny call. Our text verse for this chapter is the great apostolic prayer of Paul. We need to realize that the Lord wants us to be both spiritually and naturally successful, not one or the other. He wants to prosper us even as our souls prosper.

God's Word shows us that it would do you no good at all to *"gain the whole world and lose* [your] *soul"*:

Matthew 16:26

For what is a man profited, if he shall gain the whole world, and lose his own soul? or what shall a man give in exchange for his soul?

Having natural, personal financial success without the accompanying spiritual success leaves a person empty. Success is not the destination but, rather, the journey. I need to clearly know where I am going, but I also need to rightly identify who I am in Christ and where I am in this journey.

I believe that there are five cycles, or passages, to our spiritual destiny and many different phases within those passages. The five passages I speak of are as follows:

- DISCIPLESHIP
- MENTORING
- ACHIEVEMENT
- LEADERSHIP
- LEGACY

THE DIFFERENCE BETWEEN DISCIPLESHIP AND MENTORING

These are two different roles and functions altogether. As I am sure you are aware, in the natural, we are a fatherless generation, a "parentless" generation. As it is in the natural, so it is in the Spirit. For the most part, there is a lack of real discipleship in the Church today. Discipleship has become a lost art. Many of us were birthed into the Kingdom in some evangelistic way, but no one ever really discipled us. The Great Commission is not to make converts, but to *"make disciples."* Discipleship is a form of shepherding.

Shepherding, or discipleship, is pastoral in nature. It includes setting the foundations of relationships in place in an individual's life. It is placement in relationship to the rest of the Body. It is for person, home, church, family and career, and it's a time of laying a foundation in each believer for a successful Christian life.

Discipleship encompasses counseling, visitation and relationship. It is gaining a foundational understanding of the Word, the cross, the blood, the armor of God and how to apply the Word of God to my life, so that I can live successfully in this world. It's all about the victorious life.

Many people want to become leaders, but in the Kingdom of God, before you can become a leader, you must first be a good disciple. Some people come to me, looking to be mentored as leaders, but they are not yet even good disciples. We have to first become a disciple before we can become a leader. I send them back to their pastor, to their shepherd, to get a more sure foundation on which to build a spiritual future.

The prophet Malachi declared:

Malachi 4:6

And he shall turn the heart of the fathers to the children, and the heart of the children to their fathers, lest I come and smite the earth with a curse.

What is true discipleship? It's like David said in Psalm 34:

Psalm 34:8

O taste and see that the LORD is good.

I have tasted and found that the Lord is good. Therefore, I now testify that the Lord is good and welcome others to join me in tasting of Him. That is discipleship.

Proverbs 1-9 contains Solomon's written advice to his son, Rehoboam. Rehoboam later became king himself:

2 Chronicles 10:1

And Rehoboam went to Shechem: for to Shechem were all Israel come to make him king.

All of us need counsel and wisdom:

Proverbs 4:7

Wisdom is the principal thing; therefore get wisdom and with all thy getting get understanding.

1 Corinthians 3:18-19

Let no one deceive himself. If anyone among you seems to be wise in this age, let him become a fool that he may become wise. For the wisdom of this world is foolishness with God. For it is written, He taketh the wise in their own craftiness.

The question is: where should we look for wise counsel? Each of us, in any particular stage of life, needs the wisdom that comes through counseling with others. This counseling is normally done with older, more experienced people. Rehoboam, when he began his reign, sought such counsel:

2 Chronicles 10:6-7, NIV

Then King Rehoboam consulted the elders who had served his father Solomon during his lifetime. "How would you advise me to answer these people?" he asked. They replied, "If you will be kind to these people and please them and give them a favorable answer, they will always be your servants."

Sadly, however, Rehoboam rejected the counsel of the elders and, instead, sought the advice of immature people:

2 Chronicles 10:8-10, CSB

But he rejected the advice of the elders who had advised him, and he consulted with the young men who had grown up with him, the ones attending him. He asked them, "What message do you advise we send back to this people who said to me, 'Lighten the yoke your father put on us?'"

Then the young men who had grown up with him told him, "This is what you should say to the people who said to you, 'Your father made our yoke heavy, but you, make it lighter on us!' This is what you should say to them: 'My little finger is thicker than my father's waist!'"

Obviously, the younger men Rehoboam took counsel from lacked experience and wisdom. And he suffered because of it.

We all need godly, not ungodly counsel:

Psalm 1:1-3, NKJV

Blessed is the man
Who walks not in the counsel of the ungodly,
Nor stands in the path of sinners,
Nor sits in the seat of the scornful;
But his delight is in the law of the Lord,
And in His law he meditates day and night.
He shall be like a tree
Planted by the rivers of water,
That brings forth its fruit in its season,
Whose leaf also shall not wither;
And whatever he does shall prosper.

WHAT DO I MEAN BY MENTORING?

This is that stage in our spiritual growth and development in which we are already walking as good disciples with the Lord and are ready to progress to a place where we are equipped and empowered. Mentoring is a time of honing our gifts, talents and abilities, to prepare us for a work of service to the Lord. It is that area of our life where we are now truly the chosen. We have made a choice to begin to extend and advance the Kingdom of God by the work of service in our lives.

Mentoring can be done by a pastor, but normally needs to be done by someone in leadership who is like a life coach already. Why do I say this? You can only teach what you know. You can only take me where you have been. In the end, we all bear fruit after our kind. Mentoring must be done by a qualified person.

When God sent me to Calvary Pentecostal Camp, to sit under the ministry of Ruth Heflin, it wasn't to prepare me to live a successful Christian life, but rather, to prepare me for a work of service to the Lord. He sent me there to understand my prophetic gift and my missionary call to the nations.

What does the life of an itinerant minister look like? In all likelihood, I would not have been able to learn in a practical way from someone who had never experienced this or had a working knowledge of it. I needed someone who had lived it and could impart it and cultivate it in my life.

Mentoring is like coaching the individual in their gift, calling, career, life, wealth or destiny. According to *Webster's Dictionary*, a coach is:

One who instructs in the fundamentals.
Directs team strategy
Tutors ... primes with facts ... .
Trains for the race.

That's right, a coach "trains for the race," trains his students, or "mentees," to successfully run the race ahead of them. This is just as valid in the spiritual as it is in the natural:

Isaiah 30:20-21, NIV

*Although the L*ORD *gives you the bread of adversity and the water of affliction, your teachers will be hidden no more; with your own eyes you will see them. Whether you turn to the right or to the left, your ears will hear a voice behind you, saying, 'This is the way; walk in it.'*

It's not about the right or the left, but about the voice behind you. The experiences of others God places in your life can help through their voice of experience. Consider Moses and Joshua, Elijah and Elisha, Jesus and His disciples (see especially Luke 9 and 10). Winston Churchill once said, "The further back you look, the further ahead you can see." Don't ignore the wise counsel of those around you.

WHAT DO I MEAN BY ACHIEVEMENT?

This particular passage of your journey has to do specifically with putting your skills, giftings, talents, abilities and potential into operation and producing results. The heart of the man at the achievement level is at personal peak performance. This is the season when the rubber meets the road. This is the time to implement, activate, focus and function.

At this level, a man or woman has difficulty allowing others to do the work because, obviously, no one can do it as well. They are totally honed in on their target. Production and fruitfulness blind their thoughts, at times, to the future. They are taking their vision and provision and fully producing tangible results.

Thus far in their walk, this is the most rewarding season. The strength of the horse within them is fully running the race. They can finally feel the wind blowing in their face, and they feel like this is it. The achiever is finally doing what he or she was born for.

There is absolutely nothing wrong with this stage. It is a necessary season for each of our lives and the life of every leader.

Some people come into the Kingdom from another area of life and immediately want to move into leadership, never having been discipled or properly mentored and having no spiritual achievement, no depth or no maturity. And yet they wonder why no one wants to follow them. It is because they have nothing tangible to show that they have produced. Their teaching is always, "Do as I say, not as I do."

If someone skips the achievement level and moves right into leadership, they will never really be able to have empathy for the person who stumbles and falls and struggles. The best they can hope for is to sympathize with such individuals. A leader needs to fully understand what others are going through. Then you can give them a hand up, not a hand down.

Finally, at this level, the achiever thinks, "Wow, I've arrived!" But we all know that is not the case. This is not the destination, just a whistle stop along the way. The next phase is leadership. God has destined that we be the head and not the tail. We are not on a solo mission. We are part of a great Body, and every member of that Body is to work together toward Kingdom goals.

WHAT DO I MEANT BY LEADERSHIP?

With those at the leadership level, suddenly the achiever (or overachiever) has finally reached his or her personal goals, and now their heart turns to multiplication and duplication, because they have come to the reality that they are producing all they can from their own efforts. In order to be more productive, they now step into a place of management and leadership.

To this point, they've had no problem managing themselves and have proved that with actual achievements. Now, however, they have to refocus their energies toward equipping and empowering others. The focus is no longer on how well they can do a thing, but how well they can teach and coach others to do it.

At the leadership level, a person begins to mentor others in their gifting and calling. The purpose of the five-fold leader in the Church, described so well in Ephesians 4:11-12, is to perfect the saints, to do the work of the ministry, for the edification of the Body of Christ. At the achievement level, people are so focused on their own results that they have no time left or even a desire to sow into the next generation. This level requires completely different personality skills, motivational skills and conflict resolution skills, because it is about preparing, perfecting, equipping and motivating others toward *their* peak performance.

Now the goal is no longer what *I* can do, but what *we* can all do together. It is no longer about *my* vision, but about *our* vision. There is now a great turn in the heart of a man or woman, from the heart of the lion and ministry of the ox, to the heart of the father and the vision of the eagle, seeing the potential in others and deriving personal satisfaction from the achievement of others rather than themselves.

In this phase of my personal journey, I must instruct others, and here is the progression of my actions:

- First, I do and you watch.
- Next, we do it together.
- Finally, you do it and I watch.

Many times the best leaders, the best coaches are not always the highest achievers. This level requires a person who has the patience to joyfully walk with and work with others.

WHAT DO I MEAN BY LEGACY?

Legacy, at first sight and sound, appears to be secular in nature, but it is actually biblical and spiritual. The promise and the goal is that we will produce fruit, and it will be fruit that lasts.

At the legacy level, we are at a time of transition, a time of great change. It is a time for passing the baton. It is a releasing of those we have trained into their destiny. It is supporting others in their vision. It is the extension and advancement of the Kingdom vision we see in others, enlarging their vision and ministry.

The transition involves reaching back and bringing your experience and life skills to bear on future generations. It is delegating and releasing others into their destiny call. This is a season of delegation, delegation and more delegation.

At the leadership level, we lead. At the legacy level, we guide. The ball is now in the court of a new generation. They do all the doing, and I do all the watching, while encouraging and guiding, as necessary.

The hardest season for a man or woman of achievement is the season in which they have to sit on the sidelines and watch others pursue their destiny. Within the heart of the father, the heart of the leader, the most wonderful moment of all is when we see our spiritual and natural sons and daughters becoming who they are called to be and reaching their spiritual and natural success and destiny. The greatest gift that we can desire, have or give is to be the man or woman our parents never were, so that our children can be the people we will never be.

I hope that through this teaching you are able to discover where you are in your personal prophetic journey of destiny. As I noted at he outset, there are different phases of your journey even within these major passages I have described, when you are transitioning in, when you have settled in and when you are transitioning out into that next new season. I want you to find yourself somewhere in there.

If you are in a place of leadership, may your actions truly be those of a leader and not of a mere achiever. If you are at that season of your life in discipleship, be careful that you are not trying to lead everyone, for this is your season to sit under the heart, life and ministry of another. Your time will come.

When a student is ready, a teacher will appear. I am believing with you for all of God's blessing, for His right timing and for His perfect guidance. Let His will be done, His Kingdom come in your life and mine.

Lord, I pray that spiritual fathers and mothers would rise up and that we would have a legacy to impart to a new generation—just as those who have gone before us and pioneered the way for us. Father, I pray for the hearts of the fathers to return to the children, and, Lord, I pray that everyone would understand what season they are in. I pray for an impartation of wisdom, revelation, leadership and accountability. Teach us, Lord, to see the destinies of those to whom we will pass the baton, that they may continue to run this race with a foundational understanding of discipleship.

In Jesus' name,

Amen!

Chapter 19

MY OWN BURDEN FOR DISCIPLESHIP AND MENTORING

3 John 4, NIV

I have no greater joy than to hear that my children are walking in the truth.

I cannot emphasize enough the importance of discipleship and mentoring. Personally, I believe that this should be a lifestyle for all believers. In this chapter, I will show you why this is so important to the Church today.

We, as seasoned Christians, should always be ready to purpose in ourselves to pour into the next generation. This is what the Christian life is all about. And this is not just for those who are behind the pulpit. It is the responsibility of every person who calls themselves a born-again believer.

Barnabas mentored Paul, and Paul mentored Timothy. Elijah mentored Elisha, and he received a double-portion anointing. As our text verse reveals, John, the disciple of Jesus, also knew the joy of mentoring others.

Let us be those men and women who hear the heart of God in discipleship and reach out to others, pouring into them what God has given us. Let us be trustworthy, to allow another person to come alongside of us or for us to come alongside of someone we know is on this journey of fulfilling their destiny. Let us be history-makers and world-changers, as we purpose to build a foundation in a generation that God is raising up. Let us get ready and equipped and position ourselves for one of the greatest events that will take place on this planet.

In years past, we visited hundreds of churches, both large and small, and many of the people we meet have been in the church now for a very long time. Some have been saved for ten years and others for double that, and yet they have never really been discipled properly or mentored. Some of them suffer or are continually challenged, living on a roller-coaster-like spiritual walk. When we dig a little deeper as to what's causing these peaks and valleys, these ups and downs, the evidence keeps pointing back to a lack of discipleship and mentoring.

As we have seen, discipleship is having the foundational principles of the faith systematically instilled into our lives that will give us a solid understanding of the Word of God, the foundations of our faith and how to apply them practically in our lives in a manner that will bring successful Christian living. It's about the hearts of the fathers being turned to the children and the hearts of the children to the fathers.

Again, mentoring is when the discipleship foundation has been laid in my life, and God sends leaders who see the potential in me and are willing to take the necessary time to identify and hone the gifts, talents and abilities that God has given me and to pour into my life. In a very real sense, they are to build into my life from their own experiences and bring forth the potential that is within me for spiritual and natural success.

I thank God for the men and women He has placed in my life for discipleship and also for mentoring. I thank God for my parents and grandparents, teachers and coaches, who all laid a foundation in my life and taught me life skills. Some of those basic things, which I often take for granted, would not be in my life if it were not for the sacrifice of these people. There have also been pastors and other spiritual leaders, like Dave Gey, who was the Vice President of my company for many years. He was the area leader for the Fellowship of Christian Athletes. I am also indebted to the instructors and staff at the Brownsville Revival School of Ministry. I must always honor the men and women God has put in my life, even though I will only ever worship God Himself.

After that initial foundation was laid, I was ready for God to send mentors into my life, men like Paul Wetzel, of Pensacola, Florida, who was (and still is) my pastor. He taught me a lot about church and church protocol.

There were woman too. Principle among them were Ruth Heflin and Jane Lowder from Calvary Pentecostal

Tabernacle and Campground. They mentored me and imparted into me in the area of my prophetic call and modeled for me what it is like to be a prophetic missionary to the nations and how to flow in the Spirit and in my gifting.

There was Joan Gieson, who worked ten years with Benny Hinn and eight years with Kathryn Kuhlman. She was the number two person in the number one healing ministry in the world twice. She had a great hands-on healing anointing on her own life. She was like a spiritual mother to Pastor Mave and me, and she actually introduced us to each other.

We both had worked with Joan and were mentored by her in two different areas of her ministry. She didn't just teach us the methods of how to pray for the sick, but she modeled for us a walk of love and compassion, mixed with an amazing gift of faith. She had faith, not just to heal the sick, but also to believe for the unbelievable. She taught us how to believe in ourselves and the gift and calling of God on our lives.

There were many other people who helped us along the way. I sometimes think back on the times I cried out to God: "When?" "Why?" "How?" "Who?" "What's taking so long?" In the end, I discovered that I was the one who was taking so long. I was in the process of preparing my own heart to be able to learn, to be able to receive. The burden of teaching is on the teacher, but the burden of learning is on the student. As I said in the last chapter, when the student is ready, the teacher will appear.

In recent years, God has been taking me back spiritually and naturally to my roots—the Pensacola Revival and Calvary Campground—and has been increasing the anointing on my life in the renewal of these relationships. We have seen an increase of healings and miracles and a prophetic flow that makes me ever so thankful for those who were able to build into me a hunger in my heart for revival and for a fresh move of the Spirit.

Sister Ruth Heflin taught us that the gift of prophecy is the voice of revival. What follows is a prophetic word that she spoke over the state of Alabama in November of 1996. Pastor John Kilpatrick and his people at the Church of His Presence in Daphne, Alabama have been praying and proclaiming this word. Pastor Mave and I visited them in Mobile at the Bay of the Holy Spirit, where they were experiencing a fresh wind of the Spirit. Here is what Ruth prophesied:

Come and go with me to Alabama, for I shall make the state a beautiful way. I shall raise her up, and the wind of God shall blow upon her and through her, and the many shall come alive with my life. I, the Lord, shall be a blazing fire running through Alabama.

Alabama, know ye this: that even now the winds of God that blow upon thee shall be the power of God that sets many free. For I, the Lord, shall run through you. Run with My power, run with My joy, run with strength and bring people out.

They shall come out in the strength and witness of My glory and the blessing and fire of My Spirit, and they will say what they couldn't say before, do what they couldn't do before, and be who they have never been before. They shall be naturally supernatural and work the works of the impossible and turn the heads of the children of men.

Listen to me! Keep your eyes upon Alabama. For I say, "She shall be one that will make the news, and many shall come from far and wide. And they shall come in cars and planes and trains, to see what God is doing."

I say, "She shall be like a banjo upon My knee, and I will play a song on her that shall reach around the world. Come and go with Me and see Alabama set men free."

I am so thankful to God for allowing me to sit under Sister Ruth's ministry and have her as a mentor.

Let me close this chapter by reaffirming to you that God will always send the right person, the right individual at just the right time to sow into your life. Proverbs states:

Proverbs 17:17, NIV

A friend loves at all times,
*   and a brother is born for adversity.*

Whatever the season and whatever the need, the Lord will put the right person in your life.

I challenge you today to position yourself and to humble your heart. Let the eyes of your understanding be enlightened, that you may see, hear and know the prophetic time and season for your life. May you also recognize the divine appointments, those golden connections that God has ordained for you for such a time as this!

Father, You are so awesome and so faithful. I pray for the Spirit of Wisdom and Counsel, that as we reach out and disciple and mentor those You would bring into our lives, that people would see Jesus in us. May we exercise the fruits of the Spirit and be quick to listen and slow to speak. May we help to facilitate the shaping and sharpening of a generation that is coming up behind us. I pray, Lord, that they would be enabled by Your Spirit to surpass that which we have ever dreamed of and accomplish great things for Your glory. Thank You, Lord.

In Jesus' name,
Amen!

Chapter 20

CATCHING A FRESH PROPHETIC REVELATION OF THE LORD

Matthew 6:33, NIV

But seek first his kingdom and his righteousness, and all these things will be given to you as well.

Know that God is always speaking to us, daily, just as He did to the Israelites. He gave them fresh manna every day—even in the desert. As we spend time with the Lord and seek Him—for the deeper things, the higher things, for His thoughts—He is faithful to reveal Himself to us.

Paul prayed, as recorded in Ephesians, that the God of our Lord Jesus Christ might give to you a Spirit of wisdom and revelation in the full knowledge of Him. This should be our prayer today. God speaks to us by His Spirit and by His Word, and our spirit is quickened as we seek Him.

But we must stay in step, or in rhythm, with what the Lord is doing. There must be a new wineskin, for the Lord has saved the best wine for last. Let us draw near to Him, and let us become one with Him, as we catch the waves of revelation that He is downloading and releasing to His people today.

My heart's desire (and probably yours as well) is to get a fresh revelation *of* the Lord and a fresh revelation *from* the Lord. These are certainly two different things. There are so many different aspects to the heart of God, the nature of God and the face of God. Many of them are captured in His names:

- Jehovah-Jireh, our Provider
- Jehovah-Rapha, our Healer
- Jehovah-Nissi, our Banner
- Jehovah-Ra-ah, our Shepherd
- Jehovah-Shalom, our Peace
- Jehovah-Tsidkenu, our Righteousness

These are all wonderful, but we are also looking for a fresh revelation from Him—a *rhema* word, a *rhema* message, a now revelation for such a time as this.

One of the most insightful things that I ever heard Sister Ruth Heflin say is that when we are stepping into the river, we may step in from the same place on the bank, but we are always stepping into a new place in the river, because the river is always flowing. The River of Life is always new and always fresh, and I am looking for a fresh revelation. How about you?

If I am looking for something fresh, something new in the Spirit, I have to know that I am not going to find it in the flesh. I will only find it in the Spirit. I am looking for God, and He is Spirit. Why would I look around in the flesh or in my mind, will and emotions? That's my soul, and I have to get out of my soulish realm and into the realms of the Spirit.

In Revelation 1:10, the Word tells us that it was the Lord's Day, and John the Revelator, the one who received the greatest revelation of Jesus Christ ever recorded, said, *"I was in the Spirit on the Lord's Day."* He probably didn't have His boom box with him on the Isle of Patmos, and I don't think he was listening to one of Hillsongs' latest worship CDs. Of course, John was also not confronted with our contemporary problems, issues and hindrances.

However, I am sure that John's spiritual life was not just a typical walk in the park. Think about it. He was the last of the original disciples. He had seen his friends and contemporaries all martyred for the Gospel message and otherwise suffer for their testimony. Then he himself was put in a pot of boiling oil in an attempt to kill him. When that didn't work, he was exiled to the Isle of Patmos. His walk was, most assuredly, more challenging than ours, and yet he persevered and finished the race.

It is easy for us to say that we have to get out of the flesh and into the Spirit, but I think we don't really explain how we can accomplish that. The author of Hebrews described this process very clearly:

Hebrews 12:1-3, NKJV

> *Therefore we also, since we are surrounded by so great a cloud of witnesses, let us lay aside every weight, and the sin which so easily ensnares us, and let us run with endurance the race that is set before us, looking unto Jesus, the author and finisher of our faith, who for the joy that was set before Him endured the cross, despising the shame, and has sat down at the right hand of the throne of God. For consider Him who endured such hostility from sinners against Himself, lest you become weary and discouraged in your souls.*

If you want to get out of the flesh and into the Spirit, you have to lay aside every weighty thing. What are these weighty thing? They are the cares of this world. They are the things that hold us down, opposing our quest for liberty and freedom. And, as the writer said, *"the sin which so easily besets us."* You know what that is in your own life. It's that one thing that keeps popping up, the one that keeps getting in the way. It may be something that takes our focus off of God and onto the problems that look so big in our own sight. As noted in an earlier chapter, the spies Moses sent into the land had to contend with that, and so do we.

If we are really to be overcomers, we must face and defeat every distraction. We must keep focusing our gaze, not on the things of this world, but on Jesus Himself. Let us look unto Jesus, the Author and the Finisher of our faith. Then those things (and even the enemy who looks so big in our sight) will be dwarfed by the sight of our GREAT BIG GOD.

How big is He in your sight? How focused are you on His heart and His will, on His vision, on the quest that He has set before you? See the victory He won in the midst of all the suffering, and let this be at the heart of your inspiration.

In Revelation 4:1, Jesus told John (as He tells you and me today):

> *Come up hither and I will show thee things which must be hereafter.*

He wants to show you things yet to come. Do you want a fresh revelation of them?

Verse two of that chapter says, *"and immediately I was in the Spirit,"* and the result was that John received a third-heaven revelation.

The heavens were also opened for Ezekiel:

Ezekiel 1:1
The heavens were opened, and I saw visions of God.

Ezekiel 1:4-5
And I looked, and, behold, a whirlwind came out of the north, a great cloud, and a fire infolding itself, and a brightness was about it, and out of the midst thereof

*as the colour of amber, out of the midst of the fire. Also
out of the midst thereof came the likeness of four living
creatures.*

I rarely pray, "Oh God, would You give me an open
heaven?" Why? Because I'm in covenant relationship with
Jesus Christ and am walking in His love and favor. I am
one of the King's kids. Through the work of Christ on the
cross, I have an instant audience with the King of Kings
and Lord of Lords. There is no brass heaven above me,
and there shouldn't be above you either (unless we have
put it there in our own heart).

The Lord removed all barriers when the veil was
split in two. At any time and anywhere you are, you
can get in the Spirit and out of the flesh. Even if you
have to lay your head upon a rock, remember that the
Rock is Christ. Therefore, you and I can say, just as
Jacob did at Bethel, *"Surely the LORD is in this place"*
(Genesis 28:16).

Whether it's in dreams or visions, in the prompting
of the Spirit, in that still, small voice, or in His creation
as it surrounds us every single day, are we ready to see
God? Can we really see Him? Or do we have to go into
our closet?

Is going into our closet perhaps nothing more than
hiding in a cave? Are not God's promises *"yea"* and *"amen?"*
(2 Corinthians 1:20). He said that He would never leave
us or forsake us. In His presence, revelation is, light is, life

is, provision is. Everything we need, everything we seek, everything that makes us whole is in His presence.

When Moses spotted the burning bush, he had to turn aside to see what it meant, and so do you and I. John the Revelator had to turn to see the voice that spoke to him, and when he did, he saw what God was saying (see Revelation 1:12). Habakkuk had to stand on his watch. In the same way, you and I must press into the fullness of God, press into Him for a fresh revelation. Do whatever you need to do to get out of the flesh and into the Spirit.

Then believe. Only believe! I mean *really* believe! Whether we are looking for a fresh revelation *of* God or a fresh revelation *from* God, let's get out of the flesh and into the Spirit, and God will meet us there.

Father, I pray right now for a fresh revelation of who You are, a fresh revelation of Your ways, Your thoughts and Your purposes. I pray, Lord, that You would take us beyond the veil, to encounter the essence of who You really are. I pray, as Moses did, Lord, that Your presence would go with us wherever we go, and that we would hear Your voice in all that we do.

In Jesus' name I pray,
Amen!

Chapter 21

THIS TIME AND SEASON

Ecclesiastes 3:1, ASV

To everything there is a season and a time for every purpose under heaven.

Esther 4:14, NIV

For if you remain silent at this time, relief and deliverance for the Jews will arise from another place, but you and your father's family will perish. And who knows but that you have come to your royal position for such a time as this?

Esther was a woman God had called and placed in service with impeccable timing. Her destiny was to save her people from annihilation. In the perfect timing, she was chosen by God to fill a position with influence. She was prepared and equipped to trust God, and she entered into a season of prayer and fasting. The result was that she heard from God and was able to preserve the lineage from which our Lord Jesus would come.

Right now, the Church is in transition and in a period of reformation. The five-fold ministry is being restored to its proper place and function, and globally we are hearing God's voice in unity. The Body is being equipped and prepared to rise up and advance and take the mountains and go into the marketplace, to bring change and to take back what the enemy has stolen. This is a season for strategy, for divine alignments and divine assignments. We also need to understand that what worked ten years ago may not work the same way today.

Part of the process of finding out who I am, what I am called to be, what I am called to do, or where I am called to go has to do with understanding the times and seasons in the heart of God. As it was with the sons of Issachar, the leadership generation God is raising up will need an understanding of the prophetic nature of the Lord's heart and ways.

The book of 1 Chronicles records:

1 Chronicles 12:32, ASV
And of the children of Issachar, men that had understanding of the times, to know what Israel ought to do, the heads of them were two hundred; and all their brethren were at their commandment..

This is an hour, a day, a time and a season when God is raising up a prophetic generation of leaders who have an understanding of the times that are in the heart of God, a generation that will know His will and understand what He wants you and I and the rest of the Church to be doing.

This is the generation of leaders who will be much more prophetically related to horses than to sheep. I speak of the horses of Job 39:19-25 (NIV) that are prepared for battle:

> *Do you give the horse its strength*
> *or clothe its neck with a flowing mane?*
> *Do you make it leap like a locust,*
> *striking terror with its proud snorting?*
> *It paws fiercely, rejoicing in its strength,*
> *and charges into the fray.*
> *It laughs at fear, afraid of nothing;*
> *it does not shy away from the sword.*
> *The quiver rattles against its side,*
> *along with the flashing spear and lance.*
> *In frenzied excitement it eats up the ground;*
> *it cannot stand still when the trumpet sounds.*
> *At the blast of the trumpet it snorts, "Aha!"*
> *It catches the scent of battle from afar,*
> *the shout of commanders and the battle cry.*

These horses are not afraid. They actually mock at fear. They do not turn their backs to the sword. At the sound of the mighty trumpet, they rise up and become fierce, and the scent of battle afar off is in their nostrils. These horses represent end-time warriors and end-time handmaidens.

They are the apostolic-prophetic generation of leaders being raised up for such a time as this.

The Lord is facilitating an ingathering of eagles, godly alliances, golden connections, divine relationships, apostolic networks and fellowships drawn together. And He will now begin to release His strategy, His plan and His purposes. He wants us to go from Revival to Awakening, and from a Move to a Movement. We are the harvesters, born for the harvest, destined for the harvest, bowing our knee only to the Lord of the Harvest. Who is He? He is the Lord of Hosts, who is mighty in battle, a man of war, and the Lord is His name (see Exodus15:3).

I have said many times that we stand at the threshold of the greatest harvest ever known to man and also the greatest battle, the great end-time battle, the season that every prophet has foretold. The timing of it is NOW!

You and I, who are prophetic and part of this generation of the harvest, need to seek the Lord with all of our heart and all of our soul. All of my leaders at Eagle Worldwide Ministries, our department heads, those who pastor and lead our churches and outreach ministries are seeking the Lord right now. Join us so that He may give you the direction you need, that specific strategy, that specific hope.

During each Christmas Season, we will surely hear the Christmas story, but as men speak of the wise men of old, remember this: wise men and women still seek God for personal, corporate and Kingdom revelation and strategies today. Our God is a personal God, and now, more than at any other time in the history of man, we need to hear His voice. We, the sons of God, need to hear His voice, so that we can be led by His Spirit.

Once we hear from God, we need to implement His plans and strategies, taking His Word (whether it is the *logos*, the written Word; the prophetic, the spoken word, or the *rhema*, a personalized word) and using it to successfully extend and advance the Kingdom of God here on Earth.

Again, God is very interested in your success, both spiritual and natural. He wants to bless you and prosper you even as your soul prospers. That prosperity will come from the Word and the Spirit working together in your life.

Yes, God is interested in your success. He has said:

Joshua 1:8, NIV

Keep this Book of the Law always on your lips; meditate on it day and night, so that you may be careful to do everything written in it. Then you will be prosperous and successful.

Lord, I pray that we would be a people who know the times and seasons, just like the sons of Issachar and that You would impart to us clarity in what You are doing in the world today, not just in our own lives and our own communities, but also in other peoples, cities and nations.

Father, I pray that even as we are being prepared and equipped, we will be obedient to Your plans and Your strategies. We seek You with all our heart and know that we are about to enter one of the most exciting times in history. May we continuously be seeking Your direction for divine alignments and divine assignments.

In Jesus' name,
Amen!

Chapter 22

THE IMPORTANCE OF PROPHETIC GATES AND GATEKEEPERS

1 Chronicles 12:32, NASB

Of the sons of Issachar, men who understood the times, with knowledge of what Israel should do, their chiefs were two hundred; and all their kinsmen were at their command.

We have been in a season in which the Lord has been raising prophetic gatekeepers and prophetic watchmen. Historically, in ancient cities, a wall of protection was built around each city. The wall had gates, and gatekeepers were assigned to guard those gates.

At the main gates of those ancient cities, there were towers and a watchman there who was able to alert the gatekeeper if danger was approaching. You can see the ruins of many such walls and towers in the Middle East and also in Europe.

It is interesting to note that Peter healed the lame man at the Beautiful Gate, and five thousand came to the Lord that day. Gates are important and what takes place there is also important.

The Lord has spoken through His prophets and intercessors and prepared the way at the gates of influence for the emergence of a generation that is even now being equipped to go on the offensive and storm the gates of the enemy. By one Spirit, the Holy Spirit, we are hearing a sound of victory and a sound with marching orders. At the same time, the gatekeepers, the watchmen among God's people, are all working together in the Spirit to bring about His will on this planet.

An important revelation that the Lord had me share one New Year's Eve several years ago had to do with spiritual gates, gatekeepers and watchmen. The Lord said that He is going to be storming the gates of the enemy in the days to come.

Spiritual gates are portals and entry and exit ways into cities, nations, people groups and denominations, and even to the seven mountains of society—areas of influence, such as education, government, business, media, entertainment, etc. Gates can be individuals, places, such as cities, a point of entry, a point of importance, a point of impact, and/or a point or place of contention. And spiritual battles rage at those gates.

The gates of old were also a place of assembly (see Proverbs 1:21). They were a place where the law was read aloud, a place of proclamation (see Nehemiah 8:1-3 and 2 Chronicles 32:6). Ancient gates were a place where the priests and prophets delivered their discourses and prophecies (see Isaiah 29:21). Criminals were punished outside the gates of those cities.

Gates, being positions and places of great importance, were carefully guarded and closed at night (see Deuteronomy 3:4 and Joshua 2:5-7). That has deep significance for us all.

It Is important that we understand gates, gatekeepers, and watchman, their differences and their purposes. The Bible says that for lack of knowledge His people are destroyed. There is a battle being waged today, and it is especially fierce at the gates.

Some important gateway cities are Ellis Island in New York, Niagara and Fort Erie. Ottawa and Washington, DC, as capitals of their respective nations, are gateways to those nations and the place of political discourse.

Some gateways to entertainment are Hollywood, Nashville and Niagara Falls.

The Aboriginal people, whether it's the First Nations or the Inuit, can certainly serve as gatekeepers to a nation or an area.

Wall Street and Bay Street are places of influence and gateways into financial and economic communities.

God is putting together divine appointments, godly alliances and golden connections. He is giving us strategies—divine strategies of how, when, where and who. But we need spiritual discernment.

The spiritual leaders of this generation, I believe, will be anointed like the sons of Issachar. We not only need discernment and wisdom, but we also need spiritual understanding to know God's purpose for us personally and also for our generation.

Just as the ancient gates had purpose and meaning, so do our modern gates. They can allow or prevent entry or the free flow of commerce. They can confine, shut down and control spiritual activity and traffic.

Isaiah spoke of the Church rising up, taking dominion and authority and facilitating the harvest. In the midst of that harvest, the gates must be kept open continually so that the harvest can come in:

Isaiah 60:11, NKJV

Therefore your gates shall be open continually; they shall not be shut day or night, that men may bring to you the wealth of the Gentiles, and their kings in procession.

For the Israelites, gates were also places of worship:

Psalm 100:4, NKJV

Enter into His gates with thanksgiving,
And into His courts with praise.
Be thankful to Him, and bless His name.

Gate were a place of warfare:

Genesis 22:17

Blessing I will bless you, and multiplying I will multiply your descendants as the stars of the heaven and as the sand which is on the seashore; and your descendants shall possess the gate of their enemies.

Just as the Lord told us in spiritual warfare to bind the strong man and then raid his house (see Matthew 12:29), we must wage battle at the gates in order to take the land.

TYPES OF GATES IN THE SCRIPTURES

- The gates of our enemies (see Genesis 22:17)
- The gates of those who hate you (see Genesis 24:60)
- The gates of Heaven (see Genesis 28:17)
- The gates of righteousness (see Psalm 118:19)
- The gates of Hell (see Matthew 16:18)
- The gates to the soul (see Luke 22:3) (Satan entering Judas suggested the presence of an entrance, that is a door or gate).
- The gates to our heart (see Revelation 3:20) (Jesus is knocking at the gate of your heart. Will you open for Him to come in?)

WHO WAS AT THE GATES?

Watchmen were among those who frequented the gates. Who else might we find there? The elders and people of commerce, people doing business. The most important people there were watchmen and other spiritual warriors who understood how to contend with the enemy and protect the city.

I hope this gives you some spiritual insight, so that in the coming months and years, we can recognize important gates, guard those that need to be guarded and storm those that need to be stormed. If we are called to be gatekeepers and watchmen on the wall, in other words, if we are called to intercede and to provide protection for God's people and His House, we need to know "why," "for what" and "how." We also need to know "who" we are guarding against?

When I go into a nation or to a particular people group, I know that there are a number of different ways to do it. When the Lord launched me into ministry, He told me to look for gatekeepers, people with spiritual influence and authority. There will be times when I am called to minister to kings and other leaders or dignitaries, but first I need access to their gates, and I need a relationship with their gatekeepers.

There is a right way to go in for those who are the sent ones. I, for one, want to be one who is sent, not just someone who shows up. I want to know the Waymaker much better in the days to come. He can make a way where there is no way.

Our gift can make a place for us, and by our calling, we will be properly positioned. We need to know who we are and what we are called to do. If we learn to work together, to cooperate in a Spirit of unity, each doing our assigned job, fulfilling our role, answering the call, then the victory will surely be ours at the gates.

Lord, thank You for the gatekeepers and the watchmen. Thank You for those who rise up in intercession and are on the frontlines in battle in the Spirit, those like John the Baptist, who are preparing the way.

Father, I pray for increased discernment for Your people, that they will know the signs of the times and their spheres of influence. I pray that as they understand about the gates of their homes, communities and nations, they will stand watch and keep guard, to protect, take back and inherit what is rightfully ours.

In Jesus' name,

Amen!

Chapter 23

WHERE ARE MY ELIJAHS?

2 Kings 2:14

Where is the LORD God of Elijah?

Elisha asked this question, but God is asking us another question today. He is saying, "Where are My Elijah's?" By this, He means, "Where are the people of God who fear no man? Where are those who will confront complacency in the Church, those who are willing to stand up and be counted, those who are walking flames of fire, those who will be a prophetic voice to their generation?" God is looking for willing people, for He is raising up a new breed that will bring forth a revolution in the earth.

Elijah was a radical in his day, and the Elijahs being raised up now will also be radicals. They will be extreme in their faith and in their lifestyle. After all, Jesus was a radical too. He was extreme in His faith. He even spit on some dirt, made mud with it and then put that mud on a man's blind eyes. He did and said things that offended people, piercing them to the heart.

Are you ready to be radical? Are you ready to call down fire on injustice and sin and tear down the altars of false idols and build new ones to the true and living God? He is looking for people true to their calling, those who are willing to risk it all, those who are willing to be prophetic world-changers.

I heard the Lord say, "Where are my Elijah's?" and I knew as never before, that He was looking for you and me to stand up in the Spirit of Elijah for the greatest harvest ever known to man. The fields are white and ready for harvest. Are we ready to reap?

James wrote:

James 5:16-17, ISV

The prayer of a righteous person is powerful and effective. Elijah was a person just like us, and he prayed earnestly for it not to rain, and rain never came to the land for three years and six months.

Did you get that? Elijah was a man *"just like us."* He was just a man, but a man God could used to confront what was happening in the world of his time.

What was it like then? The people of Israel had turned away from the God of their Fathers and were serving Baal. Darkness had covered the earth and gross darkness the land. The cry in God's heart was for His people to turn back to Him, the God of Abraham, Isaac and Jacob! And that same cry is issuing forth from the heart of God today.

God is seeking a man, a woman, a prophetic generation (see Ezekiel 22:30), to stand in the gap and make up the hedge. The God of Elijah is still on the throne, and He is looking for some new Elijahs to demonstrate His power, stand for holiness and call for others to stand up for God!

In Ezekiel's famous vision of the dry bones, he was called on to prophesy:

Ezekiel 37:4-5, NKJV

"O dry bones, hear the word of the Lord!" Thus says the Lord God to these bones: "Surely I will cause breath to enter into you, and you shall live."

That is God's call to us, to speak to this generation in North America or wherever you happen to be. To do this, you don't need to deliver a good sermon with homiletic perfection or exegetical excellence. If you have a heart after God and confidence in the Lord, you can always find a pulpit today.

In this day and age, we have too many dead men in the pulpits preaching dead messages to dead people. Empty men and women are laying empty hands on empty heads and who should be surprised when nothing happens? We need to be a people who get our unction to function from the Holy Ghost, and then we must not be afraid to challenge those God calls us to speak to.

Seek the anointing, for the anointing breaks the yoke. Seek it like you have never sought it before. This generation needs the anointing. A sermon born in the head reaches the head, but a sermon born of the Spirit will reach the heart. If we are the Elijahs God has called us to be in this hour, then we will be preaching an anointed message that will produce a spiritual people.

A.W. Tozer described a preacher like this: "a man likely to be drastic, radical, and even possibly, at times, violent." The church would soon brand him as extreme, fanatical, negative and fearless. Would we be afraid to speak forth the life that dry bones needed? God is looking for a prophet to this generation. He is crying out even now:

WHERE ARE MY ELIJAHS?

We need a prophet, not just a preacher, teacher or pastor. A preacher or pastor will help everybody and hurt nobody, but a prophet will stir everybody up and anger some. A prophet is not usually received in his hometown. He'll preach against sin and confront the Church in its complacency. Leonard Ravenhill said, "Too often we are men-pleasers instead of God-pleasers. Instead of fishers of men, we are fishing for the compliments of men."

I'm so turned off by church as usual that I'm looking for the God of Elijah to show up in signs, wonders and miracles. I'm looking for Him to break me out of this self-imposed pursuit of man and the institution of "the church." Give me revival or take me home, Lord.

Elijah had spiritual children, other prophets. Of course,

he had his Elisha (see Malachi 4 and 5). That is what I'm living for, and that is what we need today—the fire of revival, hunger in our hearts, fire that never goes out and that births new generations of prophets.

Where are the Duncan Campbells, the William Seymours, the Smith Wigglesworths and the Charles Parhams of today? Where are the Pauls who are willing and wanting to know Christ in His suffering? Are we so hungry for the acceptance of man that we are willing to never know Christ in His fullness?

No man is fully accepted until he has first been fully rejected. Paul's confession before King Agrippa is the one I want, that I have not been unfaithful to the heavenly vision. He stood before the king, with his head half in the lion's mouth, and the King was impressed. He said, *"Almost thou persuadest me to be a Christian"* (Acts 26:28). A lot of people are almost persuaded.

Festus said to Paul that same day: *"Paul, thou art beside thyself; much learning doth make thee mad"* (Acts 26:24).

Paul replied, *"I am not mad, most noble Festus; but speak forth the words of truth and soberness"* (Verse 25). Is anyone today preaching the everlasting Gospel in a way that makes people call them a raving lunatic? Where are the Elijahs?

Duncan Campbell declared that a baptism of holiness, a demonstration of godly living was the crying need of his day. He died in 1972. Charles Finney said, "Revival is no more a miracle than a crop of wheat." Are we producing our crop for this end-time harvest?

Revival comes when heroic saints cry out and enter into battle, determined to win or die. Where are the Elijahs? Who will stand up and speak to the dry bones that represent the Church today? Will you be an Elijah to your generation? Will you dare to begin *Living on the Prophetic Edge?*

Father, I pray for this generation. Lord, I pray for us to stand in the Spirit of Elijah, to stand against the powers of darkness and those serving false idols. Lord, I pray for the same Spirit of boldness that fell on Your people in the book of Acts. May we walk in Your strength and be clothed with Your courage, as we stand for righteousness.

In Jesus' name,

Amen!

BIBLIOGRAPHY

Much of the teaching and material that I have received prophetically over the years has come as revelation from the Lord, but I would like to acknowledge some teachers whose teachings and writings have had an impact on me and from which I have gleaned during my prophetic journey.

Cooke, Graham. *Developing Your Prophetic Gifting.* Ada, MI: Revell, 2003.

Hammond, Bill. *Apostles, Prophets, The Coming Moves of God and Day of the Saints.* Shippensburg, PA: Destiny Image Publishers, 1997.

Heflin, Ruth Ward. The Glory series: *Glory, River Glory, Revelation Glory, Golden Glory, Unifying Glory* and *Harvest Glory.* Hagerstown, MD: McDougal Publishing.

Heflin, Wallace. *The Power of Prophecy.* Hagerstown, MD: McDougal Publishing, 1996.

AUTHOR CONTACT PAGE

You may contact the author in the following ways:

By Email
bro.russ @ eagleworldwide.com

By Phone:
+1 905 308 9991

By Mail:
PO Box 39
Copetown ON L0R1J0
Canada

On Facebook:

facebook.com/eagleworldwide

facebook.com/russ.moyer.52

By visiting his website:
www.EagleWorldwide.com

EAGLE WORLDWIDE
RETREAT & REVIVAL CENTRE

SUMMER CAMP TENT REVIVAL

July through August
8 Powerful Weeks of Revival
Every Night @ 7:00pm

Specialty Schools
School of the Prophets
School of Freedom and Healing
School of the Supernatural

Location: 976 Hwy 52 Copetown ON   L0R 1J0
Call for more details   905 308 9991
www.EagleWorldwide.com

WINTER CAMP REVIVAL GLORY

February/March
10 Powerful Days of Revival Glory
Every Night @ 7:00pm

Specialty Schools
School of the Prophets

The Dwelling Place
7895 Pensacola Blvd   Pensacola   FL   32534
Call for more details   850 473 8255
www.TheDwellingPlaceChurch.org

EAGLE WORLDWIDE NETWORK

CREDENTIALING & SPIRITUALLY COVERING

Ministers
Marketplace Ministers
Traveling & Itinerant Ministers
Missionaries
Churches
Church Networks
Home Churches
Outreach Ministries
And more...

GOVERNING OFFICIAL
PASTOR MAVE MOYER

NETWORK COORDINATOR
PASTOR JOANNA ADAMS

CREDENTIALS AVAILABLE

Certified Practical Minister
Licensed Minister
Ordained Minister

OFFICE@EAGLEWORLDWIDE.COM

EAGLE WORLDWIDE
COMMUNITY ENRICHMENT
The
KING'S
WAY
Our dedicated team of
volunteers work together to provide...
Hot Meals
Clothing
Toiletries & Basic Household Items
We also provide quality
programming designed to
EMPOWER & EQUIP
individuals to have a better
quality of life and make a
POSITIVE IMPACT i
n their community.
The King's Way
649 King Street East
Hamilton . ON . L8N 1E5
Centre 905 296 9473
ALifeAtATime.com
TRANSFORMING OUR COMMUNITY
A LIFE AT A TIME!

www.ingramcontent.com/pod-product-compliance
Lightning Source LLC
LaVergne TN
LVHW011325080426
835513LV00006B/195